MAURI OLA

MAURI OLA

Contemporary Polynesian Poems in English

WHETU MOANA II

---

edited by Albert Wendt,
Reina Whaitiri & Robert Sullivan

UNIVERSITY OF HAWAI'I PRESS
HONOLULU

First published in New Zealand by
Auckland University Press
Private Bag 92019
Auckland 1142 New Zealand

Published in North America by
University of Hawai'i Press
2840 Kolowalu Street
Honolulu, HI 96822
www.uhpress.hawaii.edu

Library of Congress Cataloging-in-Publication Data
Mauri ola : contemporary Polynesian poems in English / edited by Albert Wendt,
Reina Whaitiri and Robert Sullivan.
p. cm. -- (Whetu moana ; 2)
First published: Auckland: Auckland University Press.
Includes indexes.
ISBN 978-0-8248-3541-5 (pbk. : alk. paper)
1. Polynesian poetry (English) 2. Polynesia--Poetry. I. Wendt, Albert, 1939- II. Whaitiri, Reina, 1943-
III. Sullivan, Robert, 1967- IV. Title: Contemporary Polynesian poems in English. V. Series: Whetu moana ; 2.
PR9670.P652M38 2010
821'.92080996--dc22
2010021253

Cover design: Keely O'Shannessy, based on paintings by Albert Wendt
Printed by Printlink Ltd, Wellington

Contents

INTRODUCTION

Whetu Moana, which we published in 2003, was the first anthology of Polynesian poetry in English edited by Polynesians and is now in its third imprint. In 2004 it won the Montana New Zealand Book Award for Reference and Anthology. *Whetu Moana* is now used as a text in many universities and high schools throughout the world. *Whetu Moana* speaks with many voices and reflects the great mana'o / tūmanako / hopes / aspirations of our people who read and write poetry. We hope *Mauri Ola* does that too. We attribute the success of the first anthology to many factors and with *Mauri Ola* we hope to build on and reinforce those.

First, the anthologies serve a desire by Polynesians to share our struggles and achievements, our individual and collective everyday lives. In contrast to disempowering narratives of history and politics, they are a forum that bring our many voices together. In that sense, both *Whetu Moana* and *Mauri Ola* are collections from vulnerable yet enduring communities. Secondly, the poets, firmly rooted in the Pacific, are spread across Polynesia and the world. The poems discuss colonialism, sexism, jealousy, love of family, and respect for culture, elders and the past; they sit within a world view that does not exclusively consider human beings to be the most important species. Thirdly, the poets employ an astonishing range of Englishes and pidgins that have developed within the region, expressing the plurality of cultures, a wide range of voices, linguistic diversity, attitudes and approaches within Polynesia, which is a part of the much larger region now called Oceania. Additionally, the poetry is complexly informed by the poetic, artistic traditions and innovations of Polynesians encountering local and global art developments, and influencing and being influenced by universal resistance movements.

We cautiously use the term Polynesia, aware of its tainted history. We reclaim it as a term that invites discussion of commonalities and differences among ourselves and with other distinct groups within Oceania. For example, Polynesia is traditionally connected to Melanesia and Micronesia through ancestral and more recent family ties. As we said in the introduction to *Whetu Moana*, we take pleasure in noting and celebrating our differences both inside and outside the region. In this regard, we are delighted to see that Emelihter Kihleng and Dr Evelyn Flores are co-editing a forthcoming anthology of Micronesian writing. Other oceanic anthologies edited by indigenous writers which fall outside the scope of this collection include the *Macquarie PEN Anthology of Australian Aboriginal Writing*, edited by Anita Heiss and Peter Minter,

Vārua Tupu: New Writing from French Polynesia, edited by Kareva Mateatea-Allain, Frank Stewart and Alexander Dale Mawyer, and the Papua New Guinea journal *Savannah Flames* edited by Steven Winduo. The Pasifika Poetry website (www.nzepc.auckland.ac.nz/pasifika), a growing resource maintained by Dr Selina Marsh, contains texts and video interviews and readings by Fijian, Solomon Islands and Ni-Vanuatu poets, as well as Polynesians. The anthologies *Lali* and *Nuanua*, edited by Albert Wendt, survey Micronesian and Melanesian writing as well.

When the idea of a second anthology was suggested, we were tempted merely to revise or update *Whetu Moana*, but because so much new poetry has been written and published since its completion, we decided to compile a completely new collection. The term 'mauri ola', or 'mauri ora', is found in most Polynesian cultures. In combining the Māori 'mauri' and the word 'ola', common in many Polynesian languages, the new pan-Polynesian title makes the anthology more inclusive of all our peoples. Mauri or mauli is the location of the emotions, usually the centre of the person: the moa (Sāmoan), the nāʻau (Hawaiian), the ngākau (Māori). Ora or ola is life, to be alive. Together, mauri ola is the life force that runs through all things, gives them mana and holds them alive and together. Language is at the heart of every culture: it is what binds, defines and expresses the mind, heart, spirit and body of that culture, and it also reflects cultural changes and new directions. For us, poetry is the mauri ola of language: Tihei mauri ora! Look, we are still alive, we are still here! Despite the radical changes we have suffered, and are still undergoing, we are vibrantly alive and well and continue to define, to determine and to create ourselves and our destinies.

The poetry in this anthology expresses that loudly and proudly.

As in *Whetu Moana*, we restricted the selection to poetry written in English because within Polynesia there are more than sixteen indigenous languages, plus French, English, Portuguese, Spanish, Hindi, Japanese and others. This meant we were unable to include the many significant French-language poets from French Polynesia. It was also difficult to select from the large and varied body of poems we received – we could have filled many anthologies. As we note in *Whetu Moana*, English is now an important regional language of communication throughout Polynesia and the wider Pacific. Each Polynesian country has indigenised English and produced its own version of it: there are now many Englishes in our region, and many pidgins. In *Mauri Ola* we have attempted to arrive at a selection of poetry that reflects that linguistic truth.

The poets in the anthology come from many different island nations and languages that make up Polynesia. Some have chosen to use words and phrases in their own languages, which they feel is the best, and perhaps the only, way to express their feelings and ideas. Colonised peoples around the world are reconnecting with their native languages and those poets fortunate enough to have the knowledge take great pride in using them. Many of our languages are in danger of becoming extinct and we feel it is important to encourage their use. There is a select glossary giving meanings for the indigenous words and terms used in this anthology.

We have selected work by poets of a broad range of ages, from a pioneer generation of poets such as Hone Tuwhare, Alistair Te Ariki Campbell, J. C. Sturm, Arapera Hineira Kaa Blank, Bub Bridger and Rore Hapipi, to those who are still in their twenties, such as Chelsea Mana'olana Duarte, Kiri Piahana-Wong, Christy Passion, Sage U'ilani Takehiro, Tiare Picard, Kai Gaspar, Blaine Tolentino and Brandy Nālani McDougall. Sadly, many of our beloved pioneers have passed away over the last few years: Hone Tuwhare, Alistair Te Ariki Campbell, Arapera Blank and Jacquie Sturm. We dedicate this anthology to them, acknowledging their indefatigable struggle against racism and colonialism and to have our literature recognised nationally and internationally. We are greatly indebted to them, and thank them for the marvellous poetry they have bequeathed us. Much of the poetry in *Mauri Ola* reflects the influence of their work and example. From them, we have selected poems published in their latter years. Special mention should be made of the Hawaiian poet Wayne Kaumualii Westlake, who died tragically in 1984 at the age of 37. From his university days to his death he wrote many poems, very few of which were published. The first book of his work, *Westlake*, was published in 2009, and reveals an astounding range of poetry, from dada-influenced concrete poems to those in Pidgin. Our selection of his work in this anthology tries to reflect that richness.

As in *Whetu Moana* we have organised the poets in alphabetical order rather than by country or seniority. This makes it easier for readers to find specific poets

and doesn't privilege any one group or individual. Though we have not reprinted poems published in *Whetu Moana*, many of the poets from that book appear again here. Some, such as Karlo Mila, Selina Tusitala Marsh, Serie Barford, Hinemoana Baker and Tusiata Avia, have published full collections of their own since *Whetu Moana*. We regret that there are omissions in *Mauri Ola* as, despite our best efforts, we were unable to elicit work from some important poets. But we are excited and thrilled by the many new and compelling poets who did send us their work. Some have never published before and we are privileged to bring their poetry to the reading public. Unfortunately, we were not able to use all the poetry submitted or include every poet.

We would like to express our thanks to the many people who have helped put this collection together, especially to Sam Elworthy, Anna Hodge, Vani Sripathy and Katrina Duncan of Auckland University Press, who worked with such good grace and patience. Our gratitude and respect also goes out to all those poets and their descendants who trusted us with their work.

Ia manuia le tapua'iga
He whakaaro pai ki ngā tāngata katoa

Albert Wendt, Reina Whaitiri
and Robert Sullivan
June 2010

ACKNOWLEDGEMENTS

The editors and publisher are grateful to all the poets and copyright holders for permission to reproduce the poems in this book. They acknowledge the following publications in which some of these poems originally appeared: a poem by Vinepa Aiono in *Just Another Fantastic Anthology* (Antediluvian Press); poems by Tusiata Avia in *Wild Dogs Under My Skirt* and *Bloodclot* (Victoria University Press); by Hinemoana Baker in *Mātuhi | Needle* (Victoria University Press and Perceval Press); by Serie Barford in *Tapa Talk* (Huia); by Arapera Hineira Kaa Blank in *Ngā Kōkako Huataratara* (Arapera Blank and the Waiata Koa Trust); by Bub Bridger in *Up Here on the Hill* (Mallinson Rendel); by Tania Butcher in *Smudged Red on Cheek* (Totem Press); by Alistair Te Ariki Campbell in *The Dark Lord of Savaiki* (Hazard Press), *It's Love, Isn't It?* and *Just Poetry* (both HeadworX); by David Eggleton in *Empty Orchestra* (Auckland University Press); by Rangi Faith in *Conversation with a Moahunter* (Steele Roberts) and *Rivers without Eels* (HeadworX); by Sia Figiel in *To a Young Artist in Contemplation* (Pacific Writing Forum); by Rore Hapipi in *The Raw Men* (O-A-Tia Publishers); by Imaikalani Kalahele in *Kalahele* (Kalamāku Press); by Phil Kawana in *Devil in My Shoes* (Auckland University Press); by Kealoha on *Kealoha* (Hawaii Slam Records); by Brandy Nālani McDougall in *The Salt-Wind* (Kuleana ʻŌiwi Press); by Selina Tusitala Marsh in *Fast Talking PI* (Auckland University Press); by Trixie Te Arama Menzies in *Papakainga* and *In the Presence of My Foes* (both Waiata Koa); by Karlo Mila in *Dream Fish Floating* (Huia); by Mahealani Perez-Wendt in *Uluhaimalama* (Kuleana ʻŌiwi Press); by Leialoha Perkins in *How the ʻIva Flies* (Kamaluʻuluolele Publishers); by Brian Potiki in *Aotearoa* (Steele Roberts); by J. C. Sturm in *The Glass House* (Steele Roberts); by Robert Sullivan in *Voice Carried my Family* (Auckland University Press) and *Shout Ha! to the Sky* (Salt Publishing); by Apirana Taylor in *Te Ata Kura* and *A Canoe in Midstream* (both Canterbury University Press); by Haunani-Kay Trask in *Night is a Sharkskin Drum* (University of Hawaiʻi Press) and *Light in the Crevice Never Seen* (Calyx Books); by Hone Tuwhare in *Oooooo......!!!* (Steele Roberts), courtesy Rob Tuwhare on behalf of the Estate of Hone Tuwhare (honetuwharepoetry@gmail.com); by Albert Wendt in *The Adventures of Vela* (Huia, 2009); by Wayne Kaumualii Westlake in *Westlake* (University of Hawaiʻi Press); and by Vernice Wineera in *Mahanga* (The Institute for Polynesian Studies). Poems have also appeared in the following magazines and journals: *Achiote Seeds, Best New Zealand Poems, Hawaiʻi Review, Landfall, Otoliths, ʻŌiwi, Snorkel, Tinfish, Trout* and *Turbine*. Thanks also to Dr Mary Boyce, Naomi Losch and Laʻavasa Macpherson for assistance with the Māori, Hawaiian and Sāmoan words in the text and the glossary.

ALOHI AE'A

Born and raised in Honolulu, Hawai'i, Alohi Ae'a received a BA in English from Westmont College. She is a teacher at Kamehameha Schools, where her classes focus on Hawaiian, Pacific and world literature. Her poetry has been published in *Ruminate* and *'Ōiwi: A Native Hawaiian Journal*.

Hālāwai

I dream that you stand beneath the night
sky, watching the stars. You track
their movements, as the dome of the earth swings
overhead. The star you seek rises

and there, as it breaks the horizon, you turn. Face
Tahiti. The wind is silent at this moment. I turn
in bed; the air is cool.

Such small things keep us together. I work
the sennit of our love, roll it between
my fingers. Next week, I will help you lash
the masts. In the open ocean, the ropes we pull

will keep this canoe together. It will rise
and fall with wind and wave and storm. You go
with it. I remain here.

You sit at Moa'iki under the full bright
of a distant moon. At Waikīkī, moonlight
makes little difference – yet here I am at Queen's,
watching the waves swell dark

against a grey horizon. I catch my breath – see
the shower of light falling, falling. I find the handful
of constellations that I know. Grip them in my mind.

Nine a.m. Sunday morning. Dolphins spin
far offshore. I see their bellies flash silver. You
want to reach out and touch them, stroke the sleek pulse
of their sides. What does all that smoothness

remind you of? What are you thinking as the wind
catches in the sails? How is it that I can hear your voice,
echoing across the distant channels?

Between Bells

They travel in a knot, these
boys of mine, as if keeping close to other
sweaty, unsure bodies will
keep away the uncertainty this pubescent
life flings them into every day.

They are so entangled in the world
they've created, iPods shoved
into dark pockets, grimy cellphones
buzzing in their hands

that in the rare
moments they ascend
from self-absorption
to look around,

the smiles they send me
are unexpected – like crinkled money
in a jacket pocket, or mangoes ripening
in the October sun.

Endings

for Randy

The truth about endings is that
a thing is never really ended
Someone always stays behind
to turn out lights, wipe
off the counter, and put a newly
quiet house to sleep.

But you, my friend, winding
your way down a dark night's
dark road – things were not
supposed to end this way.

And what this ending leaves
is us, while you
have gone on to a place
we imagine is full of light
and the green of mountains
that you loved.

But we are left here,
where night comes too quickly
and its darkness lasts too long
and we cannot see the mountains
or the curve of the road ahead.

VINEPA AIONO

Vinepa Aiono is a life writer, currently compiling the memoirs of early Pasifika settlers in Aotearoa New Zealand. A blogger, short-story writer, wine taster and poet, Vinepa is also working on a collection of her own poetry.

A Measure of Manukau

Bred on the banks
– south
of the Manukau Heads
just above
– the rim
of the Bombay Hills,
I've eaten the smell
of the Ōtara flea market that
reeks of fresh fruit and fried fat
that blocks the arteries and veins
of Pasifika youth
from old age.
I've tasted soggy chips
on a foul London winter
and craved
for my mother's pork buns and sapasui
for Sunday lunches after church
when we would gather
at the Ōtara homestead
telling the same stories on Formica chairs
of life and pressure
on the end of
Dad's freezing workers wages.
Not even New York's rustle and glitz
could fade
my yearning for Manukau Pacific
for faces browned and profound
like mine, and high
on the sounds of Ardijah's
'time makes the wine'
I hum into the Manukau face of
creative spirit.

KIMO ARMITAGE

Kimo Armitage, poet, best-selling children's book author, playwright and videographer, is from Hale'iwa, O'ahu, where his maternal grandparents raised him. Kimo apprenticed with esteemed poet and novelist Albert Wendt. He is an assistant professor at Kamakakūokalani Center for Hawaiian Studies at the University of Hawai'i at Mānoa.

Once, a long time ago

by Kimo Armitage and Kai Gaspar
for Albert Wendt, with aloha

our palms had no lines and
everything we grabbed,
slipped and fell into
the empty place without
stories or beginnings.
So we prayed into
the seed of a kukui and
asked for a spark.
The kukui spoke,
telling stories of the Pacific
and of long voyages that
made the waters
in between our peoples
a warm blood
conducting voice and memory.
We were silent.

The kukui fire warmed the air
with laughter and talked
of a spectrum of tongues
that made glorious sounds
even in their differences
because our knowing
respects the talk
of trees and birds, and

the lives of rocks and fish.
The kukui spoke of genealogy / fathers and
genealogy / grandmothers who built
sturdy houses with
good intentions and fair advice
to traverse boundaries,
an ocean of stars
– to never forget
that it would always be a seed.

We are now inseparable.
From our stomachs
the kukui showed us to channel roots
thick and fibrous through our hands and feet,
to garden the fertile, dark soil,
the original callings
of our birthplaces.
We weave our words and mana'o
on palm ribs
end to end
flattening the leaves
into pages of telling
and as we are children
in the kukui's presence
there is much sharing
of the spark
and though there is measure:

I.   Our.   Duty.

We are reminded
that the night will not last, that
there is comfort in beginnings
rounding into ends
rounding into beginnings.
From the dark time until sunrise
we speak to one another
through the wetness of stone.
In our sleep, where there is
work to be done,
the soot in the blackened sky
settles into our skins
and draws our emerging patterns

into the sea,
our storied bodies blooming.

Because we are grateful
we will cry
as real men do,
while we face the South
from Keawa'ula.
We will lift our palms
toward the sun and
show how they have been
etched and written,
these pathways and memories,
deep from the teaching.

I Am Stupid

and stuck, in this parking lot
waiting to see you. The lights
of my car beam over the
parallel lines of stalls
painted in tight rows,
these white ropes are cords
taut, now slack, entwine
my stomach into knots, the
lining scrunched tightly &
acidic, the space & words
between us raspy like sand.

Perhaps we will return
as lovers at midnight
where angles & crabs
scurry into the folds this black,
a bridge across the divide
of taboo and home, the
comfort of nothingness
much easier to bear
than this fire. The heat
crackling within me. The
burn, a sweet deception.

Upon Hearing the News that My Friend Has Terminal Cancer
for Ki'ilehua

The village men
heave the sea turtle on to
the makeshift plywood table and
sharpen their knives on a wet stone.

By the time they are done
the turtle's bones and carapace
are cast aside in a pile.

I put my hands in,
feel the force
that it once was,
and understand its majesty,
this life that swam oceans.

TUSIATA AVIA

Tusiata Avia is a poet, performer and children's writer. Her solo stage show, *Wild Dogs Under My Skirt*, premiered in New Zealand in 2002 and has since toured in Austria, Germany, Hawai'i, Australia, Bali and Russia. Her first collection of poetry, also titled *Wild Dogs Under My Skirt*, was published in 2004 and her latest book of poetry, *Bloodclot*, in 2009. She was the Macmillan Brown Centre for Pacific Studies Artist in Residence at Canterbury University in 2005 and the Fulbright–Creative New Zealand Pacific Writer in Residence at the University of Hawai'i the same year. She is the 2010 Ursula Bethell Writer in Residence at the University of Canterbury.

Fresh from the Islands

I remember how he would come home
with mangoes smuggled in as palusami

he would hand them over
from his unfamiliar hands.

It was better than Xmas
unwrapping those foreign oranges

from their burnt taro leaf disguises.
He showed us how to cut them

and we took them from him
like grenades

we ran to the backyard to lick the juice
from our arms

and pick the strings from our teeth.
When we came in with our pips

our mother's was untouched –
she was sick

and tired of mangoes.

Pa'u-stina

I am da devil pa'umuku kirl
I walk down da street shakeshake my susu
I chew gum an smile wif my gold teef flashing
I call out to da good womens
sitting sitting in deir house
Eh, 'ai kae! An I make dem see my arse.

I am da dog kirl wif da fire in my arse
Dey call me da woman not da kirl
My thighs rub together make da fire in deir house
My fat taro legs my fat taro belly my fat taro susu
I walk pas all da good womens
an I laugh wif my white teef flashing.

I smell like da hot rain flashing
An all da good men are looking for my arse
All da good men are waiting for da back of deir womens

You are da good kirl da sexy kirl da lovelybeautiful kirl
Dey run like da dog I let dem lick my susu
Dey run in da back dey run to deir house.

I walk pas da high chief' house
I walk on da high-heel shoe like da spear flashingflashing
My bra tighttight so I have da 4 susu
Da whole chief' council look for my arse
An make da special fine for da pa'umuku kirl
I can hear da laughinglaughing da smiling of da womens.

My red toenails wavewave to da womens
My red toenails shineshine to da womens in deir house
I am da devil pa'umuku kirl
An I laugh when dey fine me wif my red lips flashing
I pull my skirt up an show my fat taro arse
I laugh like da dog da volcano shake my susu.

I am drinking on da road and playing wif my susu
Dancing wif da dogmen running from deir womens
I am laughing at da dogmen licking at my arse
I am laughing at da dogmen deir black arses flashing
We love you sexy kirl we love you beautiful kirl we love you lovely kirl.

I laugh like da dog like da volcano like da arse hole. Dey cry for me like susu
We want you hot rain kirl we have forgotten our womens
We will go to da house of Pulotu we will go wif our black arses flashing.

Wild Dogs Under My Skirt

I want to tattoo my legs.
Not blue or green
but black.

I want to sit opposite the tufuga
and know he means me pain.
I want him to bring out his chisel
and hammer
and strike my thighs
the whole circumference of them
like walking right round the world
like paddling across the whole Pacific

in a log
knowing that once you've pushed off
loaded the dogs on board
there's no looking back now, Bingo.

I want my legs as sharp as dogs' teeth
wild dogs
wild Sāmoan dogs
the mangy kind that bite strangers.

I want my legs like octopus
black octopus
that catch rats and eat them.

I even want my legs like centipedes
the black ones
that sting and swell for weeks.

And when it's done
I want the tufuga
to sit back and know they're not his
they never were.

I want to frighten my lovers
let them sit across from me
and whistle through their teeth.

Nafanua explains her pedigree

It's true, my father is an eel
half eel
no one said anything about his tupuaga o le āiga
and no one ever asked.
My family is fucked
I mean really fucked.
My father ate my uncles and my aunties
my mother was a Siamese twin
and there's nothing really wrong with that
but her sister took both halves of the heart.
My mother married her uncle
which makes me my own niece
and half half eel

and half half twin
and my sister
she just hates me.

Nafanua talks about her tupu'aga o le āiga

All of them started like I did
'alualutoto
bloodclot
and the only place to go was the sea
and the only place to put them was the sea.

When my breasts swell, as they do at night
I go back down
and there they are circling
like soft sharks with no teeth
and they feed
till they are big enough to look after themselves.

I call them pepe
I call them tupu'aga
(we all have to look after each other).

I heard once that the tupu'aga o le āiga live in your head
and that's the reason no one should hit you in the head
or even touch it, that
and brain damage.
The old people knew about that
the way we like to hit each other in the head

po
po
poki your ancestor
kalepe your ancestor
ku'i your ancestor
till
you're
dead

the tupu'aga come and live in my head
shark
shark

shark
shark
eel.

And that's when it comes to me
the name of my father
Saveasi'uleo, and how he ate his siblings.

HINEMOANA BAKER

Hinemoana Baker (Ngāti Raukawa, Ngāti Toa Rangatira, Te Āti Awa, Kāi Tahu, Ngāti Kiritea nō Tiamani me Ingarangi) is a writer, musician, producer, editor and teacher of creative writing. Her first book of poetry, *mātuhi | needle*, was published in New Zealand and the United States in 2004, and her new collection was released in July 2010. She has produced two albums of original music – one solo and one with her duo, Taniwha. As well as this she has released two CDs of spoken word with field recordings that she calls 'sonic poems'. One of these, *Gondwanavista*, was released in 2009 during her time as Arts Queensland Poet in Residence. More information about Hinemoana is available at www.hinemoana.co.nz.

Last Born

I am the last born
I move through the crowd with my shiny red wheels
I bring with me large animals and flaming spikes in cages
I am the last born and I know who I want to vote for
I know the identity of the figure in black
Low prices are written all over my face
I am the last born and I have a long following
Everything and everyone is my elder
I move through the relatives in my green leaves
I eat canoes and drink inlets
I have a beard and a small fat crab inside my shell

I am the last born the pōtiki the teina
Everything breaks its back over me but there are
Many ways to build from scratch and in spite of the fact
That every fourth corner of the land has been walked
Over I make everything ready, being the last born
I am desired at each event, to lay down the
Cow leather, to direct people to the location of
The demons, the devils in the tarmac
We all bite something for a living
I know not to rave and shout when I reach these places
I bring children with me, just the right number
Of pumpkins and I sing completely out of tune
Buying up all the land around with my lucky sand dollars

Still

A baby who dies in the womb
must still be born.
Your mother pressed your knee

through the skin of her belly
and you didn't push back.
Now she must bear down,

grip with her fingers,
which will feel the loss
of your tiny grip –

five snail-shell fragment
fingernails sharp as paper.
Your mother makes a fist

around herself.
Push now, the midwife says.
Your mother turns to Kuan Yin

who is eager to help:
half seated, one foot on the floor
and leaning forward

the goddess says, *Please,*
is there anything I can do?
But the room with the cradle is there;

her milk will come in
and after the incineration
your fingernails will sift

to the bed of a stream
with your skull
and the still whole

head of your femur
no bigger than the tip
of your mother's finger –

the stream,
the waterfall,
the stream again.

Sound Check

you sound just like that woman, what's her name
she sings that one about the train
check one two one two check check
ka tangi te tītī tieke one two

she sings that one about the train
can i get another tui over here
ka tangi te tītī tieke one two
my secret love's no secret any more

can i get another tui over here
at last my heart's an open door
my secret love's no secret any more
that sounds choice love what a voice

at last my heart's an open door
you got a voice on you alright
that sounds choice love what a voice
you know the crowd's gunna soak up the highs

you got a voice on you alright
had a bit of a band myself back in the day
you know the crowd's gunna soak up the highs
i'd up the tops if i was you ay

had a bit of a band myself back in the day
check one two one two check check
i'd up the tops if i was you ay
you sound just like that woman, what's her name

JOE BALAZ

Joe Balaz lives in northeast Ohio in the Greater Cleveland area. He is of Hawaiian, Slovakian and Irish descent, and has created works in American English, Hawaiian Islands Pidgin English, concrete poetry and music-poetry. He is the author of *After the Drought* (1985), two CDs of music-poetry, *Electric Laulau* (1998) and *Domino Buzz* (2006), and co-author of *Expanding the Radius* (2010), a book of concrete poetry and photography. Balaz is currently the editor of *13 Miles from Cleveland*, an online magazine of literature and art. Previously he edited *Ramrod: A Literary and Art Journal of Hawai'i* (later the *O'ahu Review*) and *Ho'omanoa: An Anthology of Contemporary Hawaiian Literature*. He was also a contributing editor on the advisory board to *Hawai'i Review: Aloha 'Aina*. Balaz's work has appeared in numerous literary publications and anthologies. More information on him can be found at www.joebalaz.com.

For the Wonders of the Universe

You may have heard: Aliens are real
and they can be contacted through the US Postal Service.

I'm looking inside a dark mailbox
at tiny metallic objects
with shiny angelic faces.

In the gleam of a reflection
a column of piled saucers
snakes its way into the clouds –
on the topmost plate
a gathering of ants are doing an interstellar bugaloo.

Cosmic sugar
like Peruvian marching powder
can get the folic acid circulating

and cause many a thorax to head for the edge of the nearest black hole.
Leaping into a prayer like a lemming
everyone follows everyone else in a regimented litany –
there must be a dead moth
somewhere near that deflated space suit.

On my computer screen
I just got an email: magnesium
is the fuel that runs their vehicles.

Thank you so much Flash Gordon
for your cryptic message –
if it wasn't for you
I would never have given up the saxophone
for the wonders of the universe.

Zen

ZNZNZNZNZNZ
ZNZNZNZNZNZ
ZNZNENENZNZ
ZNZNZNZNZNZ
ZNZNZNZNZNZ

SERIE BARFORD

Serie (Cherie) Barford was born in Aotearoa to a migrant Sāmoan mother
(Stunzner/Betham/Leaega of Lotofaga and the Sāmoan-born boat builder
William Jamieson and the families of Ifopo and Fulu [Malia] from Luatuanuu)
and a Kiwi (Celtic-Scandinavian-English) father. She also acknowledges
Algonquin Indian (Wampanoag) ancestry through the Jamieson line. Her
poetry collection, *Tapa Talk*, was published by Huia in 2007. Other poems and
short stories have been published in journals and anthologies, among them *Whetu
Moana, Niu Voices, Landfall, Poetry New Zealand, Dreadlocks, Writing the Pacific,
Trout, Blackmail Press, Snorkel* and *Best New Zealand Poems.*

How Things Change

now that I'm an old woman
I hear breathing in my head

a patina of brown spots
speckle the veined spread
of my knobbly hands

and the nights seem longer
so I dream to pass the time

last night I dressed you with
the scented heads of gardenia
strung with seeds salvaged
from the ocean's embrace

we slept on an island
floating in the fragrance
of distant mountains

and when the moon rose
rocky outcrops exhaled the heat
they'd snaffled from the sun
to warm our tangled limbs

we never imagined
our secret pandanus grove
turning into clumps
of paspalum spikelets

or our young love
giving way to bile and age

how things change

the littoral forests have fallen
and our grandchildren
speak a different tongue

this morning my namesake
drank tea with me

that smile

she was almost you

Sina's a good girl
she goes to church
visits me every Christmas
does what she's told

I want her to stay
but her heart's elsewhere

tomorrow she goes home
to Niu Sila

Found Again

our love is a tracking device
more sure than any global
positioning system

just carve us into wooden tablets
then imprint us on opposite corners
of a mighty length of siapo
and watch tusili'i spring forth

making bridges to connect us
over rock-bound starfish
scampering centipedes and
the footprints of bemused birds

we have many stories of
losing and finding each other

of getting lost
and losing others

but today all is well

I lie beneath the old mango tree
smothered with coconut oil
embellished with wild flowers
and droplets of your sweat

your ageing shoulders
still fling back proud

and I still arch towards you
like a young sweetheart

you have whispered in my hair

found again

and we both know
this is our final harbour

Nautilus Woman

I'm aware of sweat running
the channel between heart and belly

spreading into the waistband
of my too tight skirt

sticking to the clammy space
where a babe could be growing

and into this thought
a woman in a terracotta
Mother Hubbard dress
saunters and bonjours me

she's as beautiful as a deep-sea nautilus

a mollusc with an ivory shell adorned
with reddish brown stripes on the outside
and mother-of-pearl on the inside

she's wrapped a scarf about her head

frizzy black strands of petulant hair escape
defiant in the heat they will not lie down
smooth with sweat against her scalp

her loose-fitting dress is striped with
pearly lace between the shoulder blades
and on the flared sleeves beneath her elbows

she moves slowly in the heat
hands rubbing her swollen belly
and I wonder if my body
ripening with years
can house another child
survive another birthing

the woman is near her time

I can feel the drag of her babe's head
positioned to move from buoyancy
into its mother's arms

we smile at each other
lightly brush fingers
as she glides by

VALERIE BICHARD

Valerie was born in New Zealand and raised between Australia and the Pacific. Her stories originate from her rich family ancestry and personal experiences across Oceania. Her father's family stories stretch from Sāmoa and remote islands in the Koro Sea to the early mixed race pioneers who settled in Levuka, Fiji. Her mother's family stories expand from the interior of Viti Levu to the delta of the Rewa River. Valerie is a documentary film-maker, photographer and broadcast journalist. She is currently doing a PhD in Pacific and Antarctic studies at the Australian National University.

Nasalia

Still beneath the surface of the river
Speckled light ripples across smooth round pebbles
Staring into the boundless sky

Above a billi billi
Piled high with dalo and rou rou
Glides towards an evening meal by hurricane light

With the movement of her agile feet
Bubu finds her balance
Splashing, squeaking, rolling bamboo
A baby wrapped snugly on her back

Memorises the rhythm of the river
And the smell of smoky wood fire and coconut oil
On her Bubu's ebony skin

Strong hands guide the craft with skill and grace
Past laughing children
Swimming against the current

Letting go, without fear
They bob up and down

Beyond the rapids
Their laugher is gently silenced
As they are embraced by deep swirling water

At the same time the bamboo craft comes to rest upon the pebbled shore

Vu ni yalo

Our blood once flowed for each inch of soil
And when death came we were wrapped in masi
Then buried safe in Vuni-vasa

Men and women
Warriors of Viti

We lived when the world was alive with spirit
That demanded our attention

Then fathers traded parcels of land for a bottle of whiskey
With a hope that gold could honour the vu ni yalo
Poisoned by the bottle and dreams of a better life
Mothers lay down with men for money

Even though missionaries
Came and sought to convert the heathen
Superstition and insecurity
Never left the hearts of brothers and sisters

They bled the sacred trees of your ancestors
And erected shrines of victory
To men whose sons now stand to lose everything

The marking of time burdens the living
With the triumphs and failures of those who conjure the past
Shaping the present
Floating in the riddle of truth
They lose sight of the shadows following their footsteps

Twenty strong warriors are now dead
Fighting to feed their children while fields lay bare

Those who return from battle earning 4WDs and iPods
Have no eyes for a future that learns from the past

We rise unhappy
And cry into the ocean and rivers
Of their childhood

ARAPERA HINEIRA KAA BLANK

Born and raised in Rangitukia on the East Coast of the North Island, Arapera was
a teacher and poet, and one of a small group of Māori writers writing in English
during the 1950s. In 1959 she was awarded a special Katherine Mansfield
Memorial Award for her essay 'Kō taku kūmara hei wai-ū mō tama'. She was
married to Swiss-born Pius Blank for 44 years and had two children, Marino and
Anton. For the last ten years of her working life Arapera taught te reo at
Auckland Girls' Grammar School and was known affectionately by the girls as
Ma Blank.

Conversation With A Ghost 1974–1985
(on looking at other people's houses)

E ki, e ki, waiho o maunga,
Hei paepae kōiwi, whare tipuna!
Kei hea a Tāmaki-makaurau
Kua riro nei a Maungawhau, Maungarei, Ōrākei!

I built my home in shadows deep
beneath the mountains
close to where the river rippled
glimmered gave life to earth and me.
I did as I was told!
My bones now ache with
fish-hook gripping pain
from endless damp,

Mother earth no longer gleams
with kūmara vine to the water's edge.
Sewage reeks where mānuka grew,
tūtae laps on every shore
and kūtai beds grow fat, alone,
like worms in burial places.
Where is my mana now
When strangers strangle living bones?

On Maungawhau, Maungarei, Ōrākei
padlocked in by high-rise boxes
soft-silk, teak-lined, richly furnished
concrete structures, living tombstones?

Dear departed ghost, I ask you now,
What have you done to me
who followed the KAWA,
shared my mana with other people
who wonder why I,
the tangata whenua,
chooses to live in shadows deep?
For my bones no longer sing!

To A Sensitive Person

I thank you for coming
in response to my call
to play the part
of a lawyer
and an interpreter
of the many facets
of the Pākehā world!

Perhaps you will become
a sower of seeds
that yield abundance,
and have a place
in this world – of –
turmoil, that pains
the heart of humanity.

May your world flourish,
like a garden of kūmara,
and your vines reach out to
those in need.
May your family grow,
and emerge, like flowers blooming
over the wider world.

BUB BRIDGER

Bub Bridger (1924–2009) was a poet and short-story writer, who often performed her own work and drew inspiration from her Māori, Irish and English ancestry. Her writing was widely anthologised and she published several book-length collections of poetry, including *Up Here on the Hill* (1989) and *Wild Daisies: The Best of Bub Bridger*. Her writing is known for its comedic energy and its idiosyncratic instances of fantasy. She was a well-known performer who acted on stage, and she also wrote for television and broadcast radio.

Wild Daisies

If you love me
Bring me flowers
Wild daisies
Clutched in your fist
Like a torch
No orchids or roses
Or carnations
No florist's bow
Just daisies
Steal them
Risk your life for them
Up the sharp hills
In the teeth of the wind
If you love me

Bring me daisies
Wild daisies
That I will cram
In a bright vase
And marvel at

The Swans
for Jilly

Before I die
I want to see again
Something as perfect
As the sight
Of those nineteen
Black swans that flew
High against a bank
Of grey cloud turned
Silver at the edges
In the cold winter light

Their wings glittering
Their cries
Wild and lonely
Those fast dark birds
Heading south in
A long arrow
Stopped us in our tracks
And we two stood
Open-mouthed and wordless
Grounded by the glory
Of that beating flight

Remember Jilly?
Remember?
Their wild cries
And those white white
Wingtips flashing

At the Conference
Sydney University, August 1988

In the midst
Of all the academic discourse
In language fearfully
Intelligent and intimidating
There's a lady
Knitting
Sitting there listening
Smiling
While her hands fly
In cobweb-fine cotton thread
She is knitting a cloth
For her dinner table
I take the risk
And disturb her concentration
'Excuse me' I whisper
'How many stitches?'
Without
Taking her eyes off
The presenter of a paper
That has me totally confused
She murmurs
'Two thousand'

She has made my day!

In a lecture room
Stacked
With literati from all over
The world
And not missing a word
She is knitting
Two thousand stitches
Into a dinner cloth

AUDREY BROWN-PEREIRA

Born in Rarotonga and raised in Papatoetoe, Audrey Teuki Tetupuariki Tuioti Brown-Pereira is of Cook Islands Māori, Sāmoan and Pālagi descent. Audrey published *Threads of Tivaevae: Kaleidoskope of Kolours* with Veronica Vaevae and has been working on a new collection from which various pieces have appeared online, including in *Trout* and *Pasifika Poetry*. Currently living along the Capital Beltway in the United States, she is married to Ben and they have two daughters, Lisi-Malia and Rose.

the reincarnated mm: a cross cultural exchange between the big island taxi drivers and the young girl a expert visiting sāmoa for the south pacific games

read a story today
about our home
story written by a young girl   a expert   a journalist
     the young girl write
     like another young girl from america
     but girl from america
     be dead long time ago
     and this girl just born yesterday

the young girl   write like she sweet n sour or mixed up pretty yuck
     complain of slow internet
     and all talk from taxi man as if it be true
     girl write bout clock tower and wooden buses
     and island time and money to churches and rubber tyre bbq food and
     open style houses and brand new stereos and televisions inside them
     like we people aint got no choice in what we choose to do?

young girl never do no homework or study before or while she be here
     never know history of clock tower
     never know foundation of peoples' constitution
     what people fought for
     what people died for
     what a place stand for today

                    she write like where she come from
                    be so clean   so pretty   and so smart
                    so clean, so pretty and so smart – why where she come from they drop
                    asbestos in the sea?

she write her story cause she think she be funny
and her white man boss laugh with her too
no one ever think in a past life he help fight for self-determination
but young girl she never write about tangata enua or tangata whenua only tagata fanua o
    sāmoa
lighten up white man boss say
have a sense a humour
why sāmoa not laugh like ete and tofiga?
                                        young girl write a laughing story bout
                                        a place she visit only a few days
                                        she a expert on sport and taking photo
                                        not here to know or meet people of land she visit
cause she too busy oh so busy   only talk taxi drivers who chat her up and *fall her*
                                        off as they drive her from one deadline to
                                        another past traffic lights she not knowing be
                                        free turn right

the young girl   she so clean   so pretty   so smart   and so funny *[she be hilarious]*
                                        like the young girl long dead from america

she write cause she think she know truth with eyes and ears
when all time taxi driver be laughing
cause his english be *no good*
he tell young girl what she want to hear
and she so clever she write down every word.

LEILANI BURGOYNE

Leilani Burgoyne is a New Zealand-born 'afakasi Sāmoan, also of German, Tongan and Pākehā ancestry, who currently lives in Wellington. Her poetry has featured in *Niu Voices, Landfall, Blackmail Press* and more recently in the exhibition catalogue for the Tautai Contemporary Pacific Arts Trust-sponsored *Language People* exhibition. In 2006, she co-edited the book *Polynesian Panthers* and published a working paper, ' "Going Troppo" in the South Pacific: Dr Bernhard Funk of Samoa'. She has a Masters in Pacific history and has done research into the history of the port-town of Apia and the experiences of 'enemy-aliens' interned on Motuihe Island during World War I. In early 2010 Leilani received a Creative New Zealand grant to complete her first book of poetry.

The Beach

1. Honolulu

has been stripped bare
her brazen face no more
she searches for Lili'uokalani
on the moonlit shore

and yearns for the songs of yesteryear
of Kings & Queens and a time before
the allure & addiction of gunpowder
in the modern-day guise
of crystal methamphetamine

came to town. Tucked in the safe pockets of habited
missionaries with their return-trip
tickets to Paradise

aboard the gogo-cum-hula express
bound for the pearly gates atop Diamond Head
to take part in an orgy of godliness

& O'ahu weeps

2. Pape'ete

swings her wide hips
and awaits Pōmare's touch
the pig trade is dead
and Gauguin's legacy has
long since shrivelled up

Venus (& Cook) have come
& gone / along with Bligh / Omai
– and all the others

she struts her stuff
like a French mademoiselle
Polynesian bombshell
living in a colonial
time warp

unable to escape
the lure of
her own sweet
scent

3. Kororareka

is mute. His tongue cut off
by a man on a mission
with a cross and a halo
who christened him
– Saint Russell
and scrubbed his skin raw
until it shone

white

picket fences
entrap one little hell-boy
turned pristine & sterile
with his million-dollar mansion
hot-to-trot yacht

surrounded by putrid historical
waste as it seeps into the harbour

smothered by
the reek of decaying
colonial

muck

4. Levuka

snorts as he takes another swig
of his coca-kava in his makeshift
bure, with his roommate Speight

he longs for Suva
across the water
and thinks of the hot steamy
curry he ate last night

beer belly lolling
he lifts his club
and hammers at
his coup coup
clock

again

5. Apia

yawns as the mid-morning
sun reveals the imprint of a kiss
on his lover
'Apa'ula

while Vaea sleeps unaware
as the missionaries pray
the adultery of the night

away

meanwhile
the *Adler* moans
while shaking its rusty sea
bones

for we are all
seduced by the
whisper of that kiss

and the promise
of

the beach

TANIA BUTCHER

Tania Hinehou Butcher, of Te Arawa, Ngāti Raukawa and Tainui descent, writes
fiction and poetry. Tania studied at the University of Auckland and Auckland
University of Technology, then completed her Masters thesis at Massey
University on New Zealand's approach to terrorism. She is now a secondary-
school teacher of English, history, religious studies and social studies. Tania
draws poetic inspiration from her observations of Māori–Pākehā interactions, of
unrelenting urban drift and of the ever changing and never ordinary natural
environment. Her poems and fiction have appeared in numerous magazines and
books, including *Te Ao Marama: Contemporary Maori Writing*, edited by Witi
Ihimaera. Tania has published a book of poems, *Smudged Red on Cheek*.

Muriwai

On this hungry coastline
bearded by monkey apple trees
I sleep naked with the door ajar,
a book in my hand and open.

I answer the phone with eyes shut.
What are you doing?
I don't answer
but should have.

The world tugs me
and I stretch to a transparent veil.
I dream on wet sand like a tight black sheet.

Tangaroa holds me as he would a cello.
My breath covers him like a shroud.
I want to stop the sun – while
I die in his arms
on the crest of the Taiepa.

Te Tiriti O Waitangi (Oh, The Treaty)

With defences down you stand alone,
The warriors have gone home.
I heard the rumour: imperial forces were on their way.
You took stock of what you had and dug a foxhole.

I saw you on clay banks in my dreams;
stick-like appendages for arms and legs and an O head.
Ownership papers gone; gone to God.
No deeds, no 'Bill-of-Sale'. No idea, no idea.

A real estate nightmare. Back there, you said it all.
And so what? There is a gaping hole in your side.
Where is the sword that carries your blood?
Here! Beside the game.

ALISTAIR TE ARIKI CAMPBELL

Alistair Te Ariki Campbell (1925–2009), poet, playwright and novelist, was born in
Rarotonga in the Cook Islands and spent his early years there. His mother was a
Penrhyn Islander and his father a third-generation New Zealander. For years,
Campbell was a poet in the European tradition. The first major expression of his
early Polynesian influences was in *Sanctuary of Spirits* (1963), when he wrote of the
Māori history which surrounded his home at Pukerua Bay. At that time he
identified with the local Ngāti Toa tribe, but later he returned to the Cook Islands
and found a new sense of identity. His books of poetry include *The Dark Lord of
Savaiki* (1980), *Soul Traps* (1985), *Stone Rain* (1992), *Gallipoli and Other Poems* (1999),
Maori Battalion (2001), *Poets in Our Youth* (Pemmican Press), *The Dark Lord of
Savaiki: Collected Poems* (2005), *Just Poetry* (2007) and, with Meg Campbell, *It's Love,
Isn't It?* (2008). He was awarded an Honorary DLitt from Victoria University of
Wellington and in 2005 he received the Prime Minister's Award for Literary
Achievement in Poetry and was made an Officer of the New Zealand Order of
Merit.

28 (Māori) Battalion:

LVII The Māori Way

How's this for cheek?
    They steal a prize pig
        belonging to a local
bigwig, slaughter it,
    put it on a stretcher,
        cover it with a blanket,
and make their solemn way
    past the sentries who
        snap to attention
in homage to a comrade
    dead in defence of freedom –
        and let them through.
And what do you say
    to that? Don't tell me.
        It's the Māori way.

LXV Māori Battalion Veteran

I have fought throughout the war
        from Greece to Crete, from Crete
                to North Africa, and from there
to Italy. I am battle-scarred.
        I have been wounded in a dozen
                places. My mind doesn't work
properly any more. I have nightmares.
        Night and day I see pictures
                of my closest mates falling
beside me in so many battles
        I have forgotten when and where
                it was they died. I have shed
so many tears, I have no tears
        left to shed. Where my mind
                used to be there is nothing
but darkness, the sound of roaring,
        and emptiness. I have become
                an empty street in a town
that has been blown to pieces.
        No one lives there any more,
                no one who loves sunlight –
and yet at the special church
        service at Maadi at the end of
                the war when the battalion
sang the sacred hymn 'Auē Ihu'
        my dead mates came alive, and for
                the first time in years I wept,
and so did the strong men singing
        beside me. That night at base camp
                I dreamt of rain in the desert.

Cages for the Wind: XI Warning to Children

There at the bed-foot, there
where the shadows thicken
and shape themselves into tricks
of the imagination
that surprise and sicken,
lurks Māui.

Those mice you think you see
from the corner of your eye
aren't really mice at all,
but little bits of mischief
and running blind.

It's now that your hand,
dangling from the bedclothes,
is at risk of being bitten,
snapped off at the wrist,
fought over, eaten.

Stay in bed, close your eyes,
breathe a prayer,
and should you sense your soul
drifting out the window,
don't fight it, let it go.

Let the mice rejoice in the ruin
spreading across the floor,
up the walls, across the ceiling,
across the sky,
that would surely fall,
if Māui were not there to spin
his fantasies,
if Māui were not there at all.

Cook Islands Rhapsodies

for Jean and Tiline

I Dreams of Takuvaine Road

Sleep walking in Rarotonga – island
   of haunted peaks, coral white churches,
wayside graves, flamboyantes in full
   blossom, staining the roads blood red –
sleep walking, I find myself again
   in Takuvaine Road where long ago
we lived as children. There was laughter,
   there was singing, there were tears.
But the house has been pulled down,
   the childish voices silenced,

and the dream fades like sea mist at dawn
when suddenly it turns cold.

IX Taunganui Landing, Atiu

Of our house at the landing nothing
    remains but a crumbling concrete
watertank and the rubble of
    a concrete floor. The same is true
of the store that was across the way.
    Both sites have been overwhelmed
by scrub and coconut trees that have
    grown tall during the seventy years
since we lived here. I pushed my way
    through the rank weeds, and my trouser
legs became covered with sticky black
    seeds, but nothing more was
to be seen. I had half expected to see
    two small ghosts wandering about,
unable to comprehend what had happened
    to their lives, first in Tahiti,
then here in Atiu . . . And at the deserted
    landing-place the sea had nothing to say.

XI At the Farewell Dinner, Rarotonga

A marquee on Manuia Beach; night
    pressing down on the canvas,
as we dine; tūpāpaku swarming
    from tapu places on the island,
but kept at bay by powerful tūpuna
    from Tongareva. Darkness falls off
them in scales as they appear
    in a blaze of light and as quickly
vanish . . . Unnerved I turn to Cousin
    Tangaroa, who reminds me of our
first meeting: 'When I kissed you,
    our ancestors passed before my
eyes. My wife was scared when I
    told her. Now here they are,
summoned by your poems. Don't be
    afraid. They come to honour you.'

And so under their aura, all evening
   we eat and drink, make speeches,
laugh, enjoying each other's
   company. Too soon the party ends,
and I sense the tapu lifting
   as we embrace and say goodbye.

JACQUELINE CARTER

Jacqueline Carter is 35 years old, living on Waiheke Island and mother to her son, Te Whaiti-nui-a-Toi Te Reke, and her daughter, Te Au Aio Ani Mereti. Through her paternal grandmother she is Te Patuwai of Mōtītī (a hapū of Ngāti Awa) and Pākehā of mostly Irish descent; through her paternal grandfather she is Ngāi Te Rangi and Pākehā of English and Irish descent; and through her mother she is of English and Irish descent. She is currently teaching te reo Māori at Waiheke Primary School.

Our tīpuna remain

Nothing like a lone-standing nīkau
in the middle of some paddock
owned by some Pākehā
to make you feel mamae

Surrounded by maunga
who serve to remind you
that once that whole paddock
had that same sense of tapu

It's a bit like that urupā
in the middle of that reserve
that used to be a papakāinga
till some Pākehā had it burned

So consider yourselves warned:

It'll take more

than
a change of name
a chopping down of trees
a burning down of whare

to make us forget

our tīpuna remain.

Letter to a friend

Dear X,

I was reading about Ōrākei today
and you'll never guess
what in the midst of everything
Hugh Kawharu said
about our beloved Rautara St . . .

Yip, you guessed it

It seems that in the 1930s
the Crown put a road through
one of Ngāti Whātua ki Ōrākei's
only two cemeteries
and that, my dear, was Rautara St . . .

We used to joke

As to whether it was rau tara
or whether it was rau tāra
and I won't explain the difference
for people who don't speak Māori

But now what I think
and I'm finding this more and more
and it won't be the last time
I say this I'm sure

We have no idea
What was before our homes
Our backyards could all be
Full of bones

And all the Queen's horses
And all the Queen's men
Will never put any of it
Together again!

Hīkoi Poem
for Foreshore and Seabed

First it was the land
Now it is the sea

I mean

Don't forget
That these are people

Who (unlike us)

Still take the hearts
Out of dead human beings . . .

So

If 20,000 people
can't bring them to their knees

If 20,000 people
can't bring their hearts to feel

Then sure enough
like everywhere else

War will come
to make them bleed . . .

Thoughts on what's happening on Waiheke Island

It's half past midnight.

I sit on your porch

drinking wine you wouldn't finish
and smoking cigarettes you wouldn't light.

There's a storm rising.

Out the back
the bones
of a tākapu drying.

On the stove
a pot
of kiekie dyeing.

In my heart
a falling
in love

firing . . .

I don't suppose
I will ever tire

of things the colour of
blood red wine

of wine itself

of coming and going
with the tide.

And I think it's good
for those
who are used
to making

to be

in the process

of being

created

E Rongo,
whakairia
ki runga
kia tina!

Tina!

Haumi e!
Hui e!
Taiki e!

SAM CRUICKSHANK

Samuel writes that he is 'a Māori-Scots kid who was conceived in Christchurch, gestated in Tonga and eventually surfaced in Labasa, Fiji'. He now lives and works in entertainment in Hollywood, California, USA.

As good as it gets
a poem for Dame Te Atairangikaahu – Māori queen

where the cross streets collide
on infamous hollywood and vine

your star crashed into my heart
as your wairua finally left your body
from the top of maunga taupiri

roimata eyed I played hori hop-scotch
between pavement cracks of the stars
on the hollywood walk of fame

that connects james stewart on the north
across street to maria callas on the east

diagonally to gloria swanson on the west
back over street southward to william holden

ae queen, you are more than a southern
cross news story today here from hollywood

i imagined a star being cut just for you
from rarity of kāi tahu pounamu

a whetu befitting for a much loved queen
with your name etched in royal māori font

that lee smith of te taura whiri had
signed off on, for the prime minister

it was then set in the pavement of a
walk of fame that does not yet exist,
but should, on auckland's waterfront

in my mind, you were placed between
sir edmund hillary, denoting your magnitude,
and hone tuwhare, for love of māori humour

[hone, being flanked by queen sālote of
tonga on t'other side, the lucky, cheeky
                                    bugger!]

oh queen, how you won hearts and minds
of world leaders of the calibre of mandela

who'd call you on home phone direct
asking your opinions on global affairs

as you sat in front of telly, hot cuppa tea in hand
chuckling and chatting in te puea scarf and slippers.

dear dame ata, your gift to just naturally be
one's unique māori self, was as good as it gets.

iMāori

iMāori brings me the words of my fellow poets
like a 'star waka' satellite ship of custom-ised verse.

Man[n]a from heaven for the soul, downloaded
cyber fresh, as poetic whakataukī reigns to quell
heat of LA desert in a national drought of morale.

When I press speed dial, I 'kōrero our brown
words through fibre optic, networks of tukutuku DNA'.
In that moment, I'm a work of prophecy being spoken.

Yes, I'm living the dream, Māori styles, by thinking,
forming, breathing our taonga words into this world.

By email, I'm fed by sibling warrior poets whose
wairua eyes are as fierce and ferosh as my Nanny Ruihi,
our tupuna whaea, who saw first motokā in Hokianga,
and man setting foot on to the face of Marama, from the
picture box-ed wonder of her 70s black and white tīwī set.

I Love Lucy still looks the same, today on my phone as
it did as a kid at her whare. Always loved those afakasi,
cross cultural comedy shows. Lucy and Desi, mediating
bicultural reality in skilful Selina Marsh slapstick fashion,
before Kerouac and Pollock ever started splattering poetry on
page and canvas. It was Nanny Ruihi's favourite show.

Back in the day, she was exporting purple iris flowers
and kūmara to China, so what my entrepreneurial kuia
could have done with an iMāori phone, is above
and beyond me.

                    She would have rocked it, for sure.

iMāori also brings me the whānau's reo, carried on the
wifi wings of whakapapa, the toto of a poet's destiny.

Riding well the crest of this millennium
we no longer sit in literary darkness, we are inc savvy.

If we yearn for it, we should reach for it, envisage it,
write it . . .

. . . perhaps, just be what we see.

We are poetry, written down and becoming flesh.

CHELSEA MANA'OLANA DUARTE

Born in Kailua, Hawai'i, Chelsea Mana'olana Duarte is a bachelor's candidate in English and art at the University of Hawai'i at Mānoa where she received the Hemingway Award for poetry in 2009. She is part-Hawaiian and expects to receive her first degree in May 2010.

Makua

The children were growing up like wild goats
in the field
            If they got mad at one parent,
they would take their sleeping mats and stay with other relatives

There is no such thing as 'aunty' or 'uncle' or 'cousin' in this language
There are no lines to delineate biological children from other kin

There is one word, Makua. It means 'parent'
Everyone is Makua

The children did not grow wild.

The Archbishop

I approached the idols which stood upright
on a ridge overlooking an old fishing village.
The strange black surfaces were uncarved,
covered with painted tapers and strips of tapa.
Each had attracted scores of offerings:
fragments of grass, leaves and smaller stones.

A man approached, gathering cords of grass
no doubt intended for worship. I said to him:
I will bring roads and a church through this site.
I then threw down those ancient relics and tore
in pieces the tapers and strips of tapa.
The stones keeled over like black tree stumps.

Spaces

There are spaces which disappear entirely
when abandoned altogether. Houses
eventually cave in or are bulldozed over
leaving behind disembodied foundations:
cracked floor tiles, copper piping, pock-marked
concrete. Yesterday I saw a man make refuge
in the brush; he tore pages from a book,
laid them over weeds and fell into a deep sleep
with his head on hands cupped comfortably below an ear.

When needed, there are spaces. A home
with walls a landlord could easily pull
by its roots, weed-wack, rake, then discard
with other matters removed from this site.
And then, there is that space Leibniz would agree
would not exist without us. A space
we could not create separate universes for –

it shreds like a fine fabric, until there is only
a single yarn holding two great bodies together,
waving at a distance, flags after a lengthy battle.

DAVID EGGLETON

David Eggleton's mother is a Rotuman Islander from the village of Motusa; his father is European/British. A poet, writer and critic, David's publications include *South Pacific Sunrise* (poems, Penguin, 1986), *People of the Land* (poems, Penguin, 1988), *Empty Orchestra* (poems, AUP, 1995) and *After Tokyo* (short stories, ESAW, 1987). His most recent poetry collections are *Rhyming Planet* (Steele Roberts, 2001) and *Fast Talker* (AUP, 2006). David was born in Auckland, spent part of his childhood in Fiji in the 1950s and 1960s, and now lives in Dunedin, New Zealand.

Steve Irwin Way

The Glasshouse Mountains float on the horizon.
Their strange shapes fill the morning.
They are rum casks rolled down from Bundaberg,
or old pagoda bells unearthed
from a ballasted world of giants.
Steve Irwin Way switches like a croc's tail,
and the shapes vanish as Noosa traffic roars.
Daylight is on slow burn, all grease vapour
and hot air, a sugar fix hitting home.
Reptile eyes surface from cappuccino swamps,
the hills wait to speak with fire's tongue.
Gums sift light and ooze hospital balms,
my sandals feel as slippery as mango skins.
Ironic caws of rooftop crows
sound out noon's scheme of things,
waves of stink ripple through the nose.
Leaves are gnawed into brocade by insects,
bark coffins sewn for their congregations.
High rollers run the sun's lucent comb
over surf shrivelling to freckled foam.
Surfers rise to cumulus peaks and pours
above ghostly jellyfish men-o'-war,
as if to join the white-bellied eagle's soar,
then tumble like pigeons towards an ecstasy,
a rush of bubbles, the laughing Buddha of the sea.

Brightness

Along the gloss of the coastal shelf
drifts the taste of the ocean breeze,
and a perfume that pours
from trumpets of flowers.
Up there the sky smudges pastel blue,
as the sun's fire flexes
to climb like the flame
of a match head held aloft.
All the dancers of the silver meniscus
are streaming and ribboning across
green, glazed transparencies.
Epic fathoms edge their speckled
fingertips into the shallows.
Inside the cloud of the oceanic self,
soaked seeds begin to grow.
A golden comb teases foam against sand,
and the beach is dazzled
to see a sudden clarity begin to burn
through the silken morning,
leaving the world netted in light
that is caught, that is held,
and then drawn tight.

Takapuna Beach

A radiant glut of water, a marbled ocean,
luminous like the glittering green heart
of a pounamu carving revolving in the mind.

Aotearoa's a dreamboat on a perfect ocean,
the America's Cup's found in a cornflakes packet,
a runabout carousels loudly round a ruffled yacht.

Daylight's ferris wheel turns, the ocean burns,
silky tendrils of surf, all gurgle and fizz,
dry out into sand and scrunched shell.

A bounty of boutiques smelling of ocean,
a breeze is stroking the back of Takapuna Beach
disappearing into the sun's gift-wrap of glare.

Flung up above the rim of the ocean into silence,
the evening moon glows orange like barbecue carbonettes,
the sea goes on writing summer's outline in foam.

RANGI FAITH

Rangi Faith was born in Timaru, New Zealand, in 1949, and is of Kāi Tahu descent. He lives in Rangiora. His publications include *Unfinished Crossword* (Hazard Press, 1990), *Rivers Without Eels* (Huia Publishers, 2001) and *Conversation with a Moahunter* (Steele Roberts, 2005). He edited *Dangerous Landscapes* (Longman Paul, 1994), a collection of poetry for New Zealand schools. He also wrote *Technology of the Maori* (Curriculum Concepts, 2004), a resource book for teachers.

After reading Jonathan Waterman

Before light, waking in the hut
on the edge of the cliffs
at the mouth of the Ōrari River,
looking through a steamy window
at the empty field behind –
the sea falls on the beach,
& the gulls speak for those awake;

I listen to my grandparents rise,
the hut door swinging & boots on the porch;
to the sounds as paper is crushed
and driftwood placed into the stove,
the match strike & the metal door closing;

the smell of smoke
in the cold morning air

we clamber into a rocking boat,
the oars sliding into the rowlocks,

the wet smell of oilskins and
the rubber of thigh waders,
I watch the water breaking
as the blades dip & pull,
dip & pull;

the salt bite of the air,
beachwood drifts –
pile upon tangled pile,

in the distance the picket fence
of fishermen stand in the Ōrari surf
as black dots of birds fall into the sea.

First Landing

They came in cocky
with only one man for the seeing,
rowing with their backs
to a stranger's land,

& looking back
at a disappearing wake
& a ship growing smaller;

it was a quick & noisy transit
of the space
between a ship & its land;

& then they beached
like professionals –
planting the flag
& setting up guards
with feet rammed into the sand
& faces already paling
under their hats . . .

Rivers Without Eels

This jack salmon has been in a hungry river
long enough for the scales to float free:
untouched, deep, as rigid as a board
it lies on an angle to the river's flow,
the hooked jaw open,
& the eye a white marble.

There are months, they say, when the eels dig
deep into the mud, months without an 'r',
May and June, July and August,
the winter months that give the river half a chance –
might live until the next spring.

The gallery is silent.

In the darkness
two hīnaki float in mid-air
suspended on nylon gut;
the air streams past
and filters through the flax;

in the shadows, necks and eyes
slowly rise to the scent
of a fresh current.

Against the far white wall of the gallery
a jet-black eel in a crystal-clean aquarium
has given up on the light and movement

and has retreated hard into the curl
of the eel pot's lip,
the bubbles from the pump bursting
on its skin;

in the rivers the winter is biting,
fellow eels are dreaming in the mud.

With the set net cut,
the river flows free,
an elder will sleep easier tonight.

A Special Expedition

I walk the beach
with a skull in my fist;
my thumb press,
caress is silk soft
across bone;
when I return
to the cottage,
I will empty
the cranial contents –
grains of sand –
one
by
one
to the grass,
and watch the flow
of silence
and falling air.

Conversation with a moahunter
a.k.a. 'The Last Moa'

Just one trout – that's all I asked.
The Ōpihi wasn't prepared to oblige,
so it was upriver again –

following an old trail in the mist,
past the hanging cliffs where my father & I
culled out the river shags years ago.

Up the valley to a lake bed so dry
old trees, old foundations were coming up
like springs through the stuffing.

& after an afternoon downstream,
I gave up on the river & lunched
below the limestone drawings.

Hoons in a Holden were racing
up & down Raincliff Road.

I dozed. The thunder of tyres
gave way to the thunder of feet,
& beside me a moahunter
fresh from the hunt, panting.

How did it go? I asked.
Just one, he said.
Just one.

JOE KALEPO FANUA

Joe Kalepo Galoiola Fanua was born in Aunu'u, Tutuila, in American Sāmoa. He
studied at the University of Hawai'i at Mānoa. He describes himself as an
advocate, an activist and a counsellor in O'ahu communities and says of his
poems, 'I (the Americanised form of the Sāmoan collective "we") live in every
line.'

Ginger roots
for the family

It is night again for the sun and the folding leaves of the mountain trees
that shade the arid footpath worn by your feet,
weighted by popo and fa'i dangling like earlobes from a wooden yoke.

The dogs no longer bark at your arrival.

Hinged by the sound of the wind walking by
she puts an ear to the door's back
pulls the corner of the curtain upward: afraid it is you, saddened that it is not.

She sits on the floor eating kalo boiled in coconut milk,
a farmer's harvest salted with your image walking away
on dried coral that leads to the garden of knotted ginger roots cultivated by scripture.

The trail marked by jasmine grows thick against cement and marble,
consuming ivi until a familiar echo escapes the cave of the tu'ugamau
shattering the Christmas of 'avapui blossoms with dust and ash from a wife's sati,
her heart flames hover above the freshly dug grass at the base of the pua
where memories sing lyrics of another love song.

Forehead to forehead
for Moms

Forgive me, please. Neither of us are working
although he goes out carrying hope on his back,
he returns to your grandma's home silent
refusing to eat what I save him in the cocoon of aluminium foil
the way I used to see baked potatoes served in magazines.

My body is still too weak to help
but my heart is strong with prayer as I sit outside of your glass
castle. With someone else's arms I hold you, stroking your limp hair,
the color of charred wood. Your eyes I never see open up
to the sallow cheeks of my mothers and their mothers as they stand with me
against the weight of the doctor's premonition
I look a mess – wrong curly hair – strands in my unwashed face.
Three days I sit listening for your breath, take mine I urge from the metal chair,
rocking back and forth back and forth, breathing for us all.

Your eyes remain closed off to this world as your pale brown face winces.
It is time to speak only in emotions.
I ask to hold you with my own skin, to save you in my body's memory.
The doctors are slow to answer.

In the metal chair my legs extend away from me,
feet flounder in opposite direction,
my hands and fingers knead empty thighs.
The rocking becomes my chant, my 'oli to call for preparation, to pave the way.

You come, preparing yourself for the long sleep between us,
breath haggard and filled with calm wisdom.

I hold your hands, running my thumb across your knuckles,
young koa hands hold me for a lifetime. After an hour
or so, a smile rises up in the corner of your face.
I do what I know, what comes to me: Forehead to forehead. Nose to nose.

I inhale you back into my womb,
wrap you in prayer and whisper your name into a partly open mouth,
Wa'aloa. Wa'aloa, e ho'i mai.

Forgive me, please. I want you to know where you come from before you return.
Ke ho'i a'e la ka 'ōpua i Awalau.
And so it is done.

SIA FIGIEL

Sia Figiel is the matriarch of the Figiel āiga of Apia, Sāmoa. She has written three novels, a book of poetry and performance-poetry CD with Teresia Teaiwa. Sia has travelled widely and has appeared at literary festivals in Europe, South America, the United States and the Pacific Islands. Her work has been translated into German, French, Catalan, Swedish, Portuguese, Spanish and Danish. She lives with her family in Nu'uli, American Sāmoa.

Car commercials

Sitting here
Staring at the tee vee
Feeling possessive without cash
Obsessive about looks
Age
Try this cream
Promising no wrinkles
At 25
Auē!

And daytime soapies too
And talk shows too
Not to mention car commercials
Selling engines with permanently youthful
Blondes in bikinis smiling
At my obsessions
My lack of worldly possessions
Auē!

I wonder
If the blondes
Have three-year guarantees
That they too won't rust
In tropical climates . . . ???

Dawn approaching I think of a friend
to another globetrotter

so here i am at
4 o'clock in the morning
at the inter-continental
looking out to the lights of Sydney
the harbour bridge
the opera house
that pointy thing
and they've put me on the
14th floor
so you can imagine how
i feel
and i can imagine how you
felt
and the silence does become
more acute
(like you said it would be)
sitting here
alone
at 4 o'clock in the morning
remembering the last time i
saw you laugh
mad-dog
sad-dog
baaaad dog suva
famished we were
after an after
noon of poetry
and conversation

feminism
wo-manism
nephews

our Mothers

expectations
and frequent flying programmes too
and the poems we
write
in hotel rooms

may these poems i write
now
find their way to you
in feejee
at u
s-pee
(as i hope
they will)

and in returning
they might bring the scent of
moso'oi
the one you wear in the bun
in your hair
to calm these inter-
continental
fears
of falling from this room
that stop me from sleep

it is 4 o'clock in the morning Konai
4 o'clock
and the room like you said it would be
is quiet
is quiet
is quiet
awaiting
the approaching dawn

The daffodils – from a native's perspective

Apologies Mr
Wordsworth
But I too wandered
Lonely as
A cloud
When I first heard your
Little poem
Form three
Literature class
That floats on high
O'er vales
And hills
She made us me
Morise you
Along with tiger!
Tiger!
Burning bright!
In the forest
Of your other
19th-century
Roman
Tic friends
When all at once
She'd pull my ear
Each time
I stared
At the auke bush
Next to the mango tree
Outside
But in the end I
Became quite the expert
On your host of golden daffodils beside the lake beneath
The trees fluttering and dancing
Under the pulu tree
Singing
Singing
The Daffodils
Your precious daffodils
My precious
Daffodils
My *only* possession
At 15

The one thing
I didn't have to
Share
Not knowing what
Was fluttering
What
Was dancing
But
Never mind
Whatever they must have been
They must have
Been magical
Enchanting even
Because they
Too
Put a smile
On my face
Whenever
I lie
On my mat
Oft
In pensive mood
Trying to find
Some bliss
Of solitude
Now
And then
Without the dogs
The roosters
The āiga
My āiga
The village
My village
The district
My district
The neighbours
The neighbours' radio
Their TV
Their big mouth Aunty who swears all the time at the
kids because they haven't started the saka and it's
already five o'clock in the evening God I hate that
woman but smile at her anyway – the only way to watch
Days of our Lives . . .
Do

You
Know
What
I
Mean
Mr
Words
Worth?
Do
You
Know
What
I
Mean?

KAI GASPAR

Kai is from Hōnaunau on the Big Island of Hawai'i and likes animals.

The Broken Pounder

Pōhaku ku'i 'ai
A pig found you
hidden in the old wall
cradled from the heat of the sun
Born again like the 'ili'ili hānau o Kōloa

Pōhaku ku'i 'ai
you are halved
but the spirit remains
It knows the hands of men
their industry
their smells of survival and celebration:
the blistered hair of the pua'a

the warm flesh of the kalo, the 'uala
You were thanked in the intricate
mesh of things

Pōhaku ku'i 'ai
who took care of families, villages
with your hard belly pressed
against the papa ku'i
the excited release as muscle and stone
fell together, rose together
infused with prayers of the lo'i:
may this land be blessed with a deep bounty
grant me life
grant my family life
grant all who seek our hospitality life

Pōhaku ku'i 'ai
Now you are paralysed
virility spent into shadow
but your spirit remains
You are delivered to me
and I will take care of you

The Visitor

Four days here and already the heat and the food
and the life makes her stomach swell.
The tank water with the mosquitoes skimming the surface
makes her face crumple.
The propane gas to make her breakfast
keeps her in the other room.
The sounds of our dream breathing and flutter
of the banana trees and dropping fruit
in the dark damp keeps her from resting.

While I pull weeds in the afternoon
when the sun rests down by Ka'awaloa
she waits inside with her delicate skin
and tells the children stories of when we were girls
with pretty dresses and plenty of laughter in our hearts.
When they tell me, smiling, Aunty said this, Aunty said that
I nod and know that's not how it happened.

My car is a mountain car filled with baskets
of dirty clothes and obedient children,
grumbling even after a fill-up at Shimizu's.
We grab boiled eggs and apple juice
and putter to Caps Laundry where the whir of machines
competes with the gossip of big Polynesian mothers,
the squeals of scurrying children
who look for quarters in lint traps.
I introduce my sister to everyone while I help fold sheets,
careful to keep them from touching the ground,
and there are quiet hellos and no touching and no kisses
before she returns to our clothes, spiralling
behind the heated glass.
Zippers whack the metal violently
as she stares puzzled by my laughter, my quick talking,
my hands moving and touching the other women.

I order loco mocos and french fries that come
in mustard-colored paper spotted with oil.
I give the children quarters for video games.
They hug me with sticky fingers
and hide ketchup packets in their clothes.
My sister asks me how I know those women
and what language I was speaking.
I laugh and tell her it's English.
She lifts her eyebrows and stops eating after two bites.
She puts her arms around her stomach,
squeezes her eyes shut, and a small noise escapes.
When I wrap up the food to take home she tells me
I have no shame and quickly throws the food into the rubbish.

Evening comes and this is the only time she'll bathe
in the aluminium tub outside.
She covers her breasts and her vagina as she sits
and I pour hot water over her neck.
She stares into the forest, looking for sneaky eyes.
I assure her there's no one out there, but she says
the Japanese man down the road has a look.
He's Filipino I tell her and he brings me honey
from his farm and Tupperware full of pansit.
She puts her hand on her stomach and asks
when I'm coming home because I don't look like
a woman who shits in a hole forever.
I rub her back with a soapy cloth.

I trust my mountain car on the weekend
to take us down to the Kona Surf disco
where the tourists smell like a department store.
We drink and laugh with good-looking men
and my sister tells stories of high school
that aren't her stories, they're mine.
But I let her go while I cruise with the waitress
who I used to clean houses with.
Soon my sister begins to dance and chant
'wiki wacky' loudly and the men laugh
because she's beautiful and smells like them.
She points at me and yells 'You should hear her
talk Hawaiian. She acts just like one.
Say something in that talk!'
When I drag her back to the car she knows
I'm never going back with her.
She looks at my eyes, which are her eyes too,
and asks 'Why do you want to stay so much?
You're like a white nigger here.'
When she sees my fist coming
she squeals and shuts her eyes.

The ride up the mountain is blue and quiet.
At home I lie on the floor watching the low kerosene
light make my children's faces look alive.
I think of what she said and her words are foul.
The way I talk and the words that make my thoughts
change all the time, and it's always me,
and it's always respectful.

Rain starts on the tin roof and I watch the back
of my sister's head, pressed close to the wall.
Her legs are folded and her arms wind around her belly.
I go to her and we don't talk.
I roll her on to her stomach and I climb on top
so that my weight and fingers press into her back.
Soon the flatulence comes and comes
but I don't move because there's no shame here.

MAREWA GLOVER

Marewa Glover (Ngā Puhi) writes: 'energy and time seems to be finite: loving competes and wins over creative writing. Raising a daughter now, working full time as director of the Centre for Tobacco Control Research at the University of Auckland, and teaching and mentoring students. Writing is mostly academic lately. I'm using Facebook, Twitter and a blog as outlets to remind me to continue to write bravely, poetically, politically.'

Saturday

It's a whip-round storm
determined to wet everywhere
demanding attention
with the biggest thunder
chilling with cold
wind slapping from every direction
It's one of those storms
for couples and new lovers
a stay-in-bed storm
to cuddle up by, and
fuck all day to . . .

MICHAEL GREIG

Michael Greig was born in Nelson, New Zealand, in 1953. His heritage includes
Northern Cook Island, Scottish, English, Jewish and Portuguese elements.
Trained as a medical laboratory technologist, he is still learning new skills in
many diverse trades. Greig has had work published in *Visions of the Pacific* (6th
Festival of Pacific Arts) and in Pacific Island newspapers, including the *Cook
Island Press* and the *Cook Island Star* and is involved in performance poetry,
contemporary traditional storytelling and tango.

Tango

Why do you dance Tango, Uncle?
It is not culturally appropriate, not PC for PIs.

I dance in memory for the past, the lost, those taken by
the Blackbirders, like Koria on Rakahanga, and those
from Tongareva lost to the slavers from Peru.

In a far off land removed from the light and pleasant
breeze that makes the fronds of the coconut planted by Hiuku
dance, 'Aue, Tera paa te Uru avatea,
Te fahirihiri i te maru o Araiava?'

Now generations later, where is the contact with these
our family, separated in time, in distance but connected
in loss, souls searching for identity?

Tango was the dance that evolved with the dispossessed
and lost. We merge with the melancholy of the music,
the words, the beat, and the melody.
With eyes closed and in close embrace we seek that
moment of escape to that perfect Tango moment.
A Zen moment of detachment, seeking, seeking.

I dance to remember.
I dance to find.

RORE HAPIPI

Born in 1935 in Ōruanui, north of Taupō, Rore Hapipi has worked at numerous jobs (mainly manual) throughout New Zealand, though he is now retired and living again in his home town. He has published poems, stories, articles and plays in numerous magazines and anthologies, including *Te Ao Hou, Te Maori, Landfall, Mate, Arena*, the *New Zealand Listener, Contemporary Maori Writing, Into the World of Light* and *Te Ao Marama* (vol. 1), dating back to the mid-1950s. He was awarded the Maori Affairs Writer's Award in 1975, won the Feltex Award for the best television script for 1981, and was the Katherine Mansfield Menton Fellow for 1984. His most recent books are *Piko Piko Pickin' Blues* (O-A-Tia Publishers, 2005) and *The Raw Men: Selected Poems 1954–2005, Volume 1* (O-A-Tia Publishers, 2006).

Māori Land Protest March

They will be gathering at the marae's periphery now.
Most will be limping from blistered feet
or aching muscles. (It was my ankle that troubled me.)
But some will be strong still, prepared to walk all night

if called to. These ones looked frighteningly indestructible
as you walked along behind them, trying not to limp.
Yet you had to admit a growing admiration.
In the last long twilight of days' end

they will be filing into the wharepuni to the mihi-hongi
of the tangata whenua, grateful to sit down on the hard forms
put out for them (embarrassed by the toe-jam stink
of their sweating feet) under the scrutinising eyes

of the kaumātua (bland looks that gradually give way
to open admiration). I gulped back a cry, the first night
after I left them; felt dead for a long time, then realised
my heart was still there. It was the best I could do

e hoa mā, put my feet where my heart was.
As it was I stayed a day longer than I'd intended.
For I am caught up in the compromise of suburban domesticity.
So here I am sitting in front of my television set.

The aches of the walk are gone now before the lit lounge fire.
But I'll be back soon to claim my heart.

Eastbourne, Wellington, September 1975

Waiata Tangi
A Lament for the Premature Death of Dr Maharaia Winiata

I hear a grieving throughout the land,
soft as the murmuring of the wind in the trees;
barely audible. Is it the women of my race keening
for the dead? Or is it, after all, only the wind
murmuring in the trees and playing tricks on my ears?

Yet surely, I hear a grieving throughout the land,
wafted to me from the many marae of my People;
the wailing of our women for the departing souls of
great rangatira, as they pass on their way to
Te Rerenga Wairua, down through the history of my Race.
For today a rangatira passed away, prematurely;
cut down in mid-stride. His promise unfulfilled.

Is this then, the reason for the keening I imagine I now hear?
Or are they grieving for we who are left behind?
(For we needed such a man.)

I hear a grieving throughout the land
soft as the murmuring of the wind in the trees.
Or is it only the murmuring of the wind,
for my ears alone to hear?

'Flockhouse', Bulls, 1962

Tame Iti
Behind the tattooed face

I remember when we first met. That time at Hemi's tangi.
'Tēnā koe' I said. 'Tēnā koe' you replied.
You drew your short, stocky frame up to its full height
when we embraced; bearhugged in the way Hemi had made popular.

(The pressing of noses wasn't in vogue then. Nor was
the full tattooing of the face.) Holding each other for a long time
in silent acknowledgement of the sad occasion. But also, I think,
in recognition of a kindred spirit and an unspoken sorrow
that went back deeper than the occasion.

And after, when we drew apart, holding the other at arm's length
while we searched each other's eyes for some confirmation
of this, I found myself looking into the softest, warmest,
most sensitive eyes I have ever looked into.

I had, of course, heard of you, from when you were arrested
on Parliament Grounds, that time.

Much water has flowed under the bridge since, e hoa.
Our lives gone their separate ways. And, if mine, in the meantime,
has travelled the more conventional road to suburban sedateness,
yours has become the recognisable face of the feared activist,
with its ferocious adornments since acquired.

So it was with some apprehension that; on spotting each other
across the grounds at Eva's recently, we approached to greet;
to acknowledge recognition of each other. Wondering
what I would now see in the eyes half hidden behind the savage
mask. If the aroha I recalled would now be replaced
by an indifferent rage, even hatred!

'Tēnā koe e hoa' you said (the voice, at least, was that,
that I recalled. The distinctive, husky, warm timbre.).
'Tēnā koe Tame' I replied, as we leaned in towards each other,
eyes closed, to offer our noses and foreheads in that intimate way
that kindred spirits acknowledge one another (the pressing
of noses in the hongi being in vogue now), aware of the
emanations of that proximate famous tattooed face.

As it turned out, my fear was unfounded. For, as we drew apart,
holding the other at arm's length, while we searched
each other's eyes for further confirmation of what we felt
all those years ago, I found myself again, looking into
the softest, warmest, most sensitive eyes I have ever looked into.

Taupō, October 1997

AROHA HARRIS

Aroha Harris belongs to Te Rarawa and Ngā Puhi iwi, and is a lecturer at the
University of Auckland History Department.

How She Knows She is Māori: a checklist

I ask her where she is from.
She answers like I want to know
why her island, beach, valley, hilltop
is the only place in the world
that really matters,
like it really matters.

Someone told her
she doesn't look
Māori.

We talk children.
She tells me about her nephew
born on an incoming tide,
high prince of the kōhanga reo
with its higgledy-piggledy
loose family units.

Someone said her name
doesn't sound
Māori.

We eat drink.
She frowns at oysters slurped
boisterously from their shells,
jokes she's not that kind of Māori,
but boy can she put those kinas away,
we both like trim latte two equals.

Someone laughed
she is middle-class
Māori.

We hear speeches.
She thrusts her political eyes
into the fray,
Māori tongues slice and dice
her Māori heart,
she bleeds in other languages.

Someone swelled
she is clever
Māori.

Her name is alice, sarah, irene
someone calls her aunty
someone calls her cuz
she is Tūhoe, Te Āti Awa, Ngāi Te Rangi
she is fair, she knows
she is her own
checklist.

Kina

You came to me from friends
wet with the Hokianga and
smiling.

Now
fattened slice of orange moon
slip from teaspoon to tongue
in holiest communion.

Nau mai and āmine
oh sweet sweet reminder of
the delicacy of life.

KU'UALOHA HO'OMANAWANUI

Ku'ualoha Ho'omanawanui is a Kanaka Maoli poet, artist, and mālama 'āina advocate. She is also a founding and current chief editor of '*Ōiwi: A Native Hawaiian Journal.* She has widely published both critical essays and creative writing in Hawai'i and abroad. She was born in Kailua, O'ahu, and raised in Wailua Homesteads, Kaua'i, and has been a Ko'olau east-side girl her whole life, currently dividing her time between Anahola, Kaua'i and Ha'ikū, O'ahu.

Tatz

Da bois write tatz
all up dea ahm
down da thigh
across dea backz
tappin experience
into dea skin
like genealogy
dea personal history
names of dead ancestors
tapped into skin
inoa pō mix wit blood
invisible dna
made visible
dey cahv images of ancestahs
like kalo
hahts wit dea ipo's namez
love an ancestry tapped
tru tūtū's sewing needle
wrapped in cotton tred
like
dey no moa pepa in da house
like
dey scade fo'get something
like
who dey are
wea dey come from
wea dey stay
wea dey goin

cuz
mo'olelo fade wit memory
so
mix ink wit blood wit pain
equal
no fo'get

IMAIKALANI KALAHELE

An artist, poet and political activist, Imaikalani Kalahele was born in Hawai'i in 1950. He is a graduate of McKinley University and currently lives in Kalihi on the island of O'ahu.

Ē Laka Ē

Famous are you Laka.
Laka the Storyteller,
   the Documentor,
   the Historian.

Ē Laka Ē
   Laka of the Forest,
   The Tree-Cutter,
   The Chip-Maker.

Ē Laka Ē
E Kū Mau Mau.
   Laka our Sister.
   Laka our Brother.
   Laka Dancer-Through-Time

   Ē Laka Ē
   Ē Laka Ē
   Ē Laka Ē.

Make Rope

get this old man
he live by my house
he just make rope
every day
you see him making rope
if
he not playing his 'ukulele
or
picking up his mo'opuna
he making
rope

and nobody wen ask him
why?
how come?
he always making
rope

morning time . . . making rope
day time . . . making rope
night time . . . making rope
all the time . . . making rope

must get enuf rope
for make Hōkūle'a already

most time
he no talk
too much
to nobody

he just sit there
making rope

one day
he was partying by
his house
you know
playing music
talking stink
about the other
guys them

I was just
coming out of the bushes
in back the house
and
there he was
under the mango tree
making rope
and he saw me

all shame
I look at him and said
'Aloha Papa'
he just look up
one eye
and said
'Howzit! What? Party?
Alright!'

I had to ask
'E kala mai, Papa
I can ask you one question?

'How come
every day you make rope
at the bus stop
you making rope
outside McDonald's drinking coffee
you making rope.
How come?'

e wen
look up again
you know
only the eyes move kine
putting one more
strand of coconut fibre
on to the kaula
he make one
fast twist
and said
'The kaula of our people
is 2000 years old
boy
some time . . . good

some time . . . bad
some time . . . strong
some time . . . sad
but most time
us guys
just like this rope

'one by one
strand by strand
we become
the memory of our people
and
we still growing
so
be proud
do good

'and
make rope
boy
make rope.'

A Letter to My Brother

Where does the sun set
Is it here? Is it there?
I know it was somewhere

Perhaps a storm came
and the stream
washed it away?

Perhaps the mountains
came down on us
and covered it all up?

Maybe it was the kai.
Maybe the kai came up
and flooded the valleys
and on its way back
when hāpai everything
and take it all out to sea.

Nah, bra,
it wasn't any of these things.
The storm was greed,
swelling like a dammed-up stream
making ready to over run
and wash away.

And the mountains that crumbled
did so because of absence.
Absence from the land.
Absence from the kai.
Absence from the people.
Absence from the mana.

And we know what the wave was!
Genocide.
Flooding the valleys
and stripping the limu clean
from the rocks.
Sweeping away the 'ōpae
from the streams,
the 'ulu from the land
and the maoli from the earth.

So . . . ah . . . tell me, brah,
where does the sun set?
Is it here?
Is it there?
Oh . . . ah . . . tell me
where do I take Granpa's bones?

School Street Bridge

Small kid time my brother Bully when carry me on his back to the middle of Waikahalulu. And there he taught me to swim. Today I walk past that pond. Even more polluted than before, down past the 'ele'ele cement slide with the broken bottles and empty beer cans, under the School Street bridge. I discover mountains of cement canvases painted with the songs of the young. Spooky music, bra, spooky music.

Kaho'olawe

My brother George
your voice
will always live
on the winds of change,
E mau ka Maoli!
And damn to hell
the puni kālā
that came and took you.
       ha

PHIL KAWANA

Phil Kawana was born in Hawera, New Zealand, in December 1965. Of Ngā Ruahinerangi, Ngāti Ruanui and Ngāti Kahungunu ki Wairarapa descent, his whakapapa also includes Scots and English. Originally known as a short-story writer, having released two critically acclaimed collections *Dead Jazz Guys* (Huia, 1996) and *Attack of the Skunk People* (Huia, 1999), since 2002 he has focused on poetry. This led to his first solo poetry collection, *The Devil in my Shoes* (AUP, 2005). Phil's work has been widely anthologised and broadcast, and is also taught in secondary and tertiary courses in New Zealand, North America, Asia and Europe. A short-film version of his story 'Redemption' screened at the Berlin Film Festival early in 2010. Phil currently lives in Wellington, in poetically correct squalor.

Adrift

What is there for us to do,
now that the stars have been
filleted from the sky, leaving
only pale clouds peeled back from
the night's dark flesh?
No tales or tīpuna to guide our way.
Shall we cast our dreams upon the sea
or chain them to our feet, wait and
drift, praying for salvation?

Sometimes we hear cries, deep
in the belly of the night. Seabirds?
Kaitiaki? The imagined songs of
an imagined people?

Perhaps it is the sound
of departing spirits, or merely
the salt wind hunting
the discarded stars.

Evolution

As I rise unsteady from the sea
and the world that once confined me falls away,
my breath falters in this unfamiliar air.
Help me breathe, guide my eye towards new horizons.
When I have plotted a new course, will you
set me on my way with the sun at my back?
I will break one cycle to create another.
All things shall continue to revolve and rotate
inexorably towards their varied ends.

And eventually the scales will fall
from my sides, will dance like angels decked with tinsel.
Gods and demigods comb back the sea's hair
and fasten raukura to the clouds.

My scales are gone, my fins have mutated,
the beginnings of legs shuffle
up the shore towards shelter
from the eyes of scavengers.

How to Train Your Labourer

She obviously thought
he was simple. After all
he was there to move her
office furniture.
How smart could he be?
And since he worked
so hard and so well,
she thought she should offer
some kind of encouragement.

'Would you like a pastry?'
she asked, holding a fresh Danish
in her outstretched fingertips.

He looked at her for a second,
barked, then lay on his back
and waited for a tummy rub.

Urupā

We face the mountain.
The headstones are pale imitations
   of the sleeping maunga.
It is waiting, biding its time.
The land around us was seized
   and sold years ago;
the cord was cut, and we were set adrift
   into a strange new world.
We were born, we live,
   and we shall die.
I hope when the wait's over,
   when I follow Taranaki into sleep,
that there will be someone left
   to maintain the fence
     that keeps the sheep from my grave.

DAVID KEALI'I

David Keali'i is a Queer Kanaka Maoli poet who was born and raised in
Springfield, Massachusetts. In 2009 he represented the city of Worcester along
with four other poets at the National Poetry Slam. His poems have appeared in or
are forthcoming from: 'Ōiwi: A Native Hawaiian Journal, Full of Crow and Mythium:
The Journal of Contemporary Literature and Cultural Voices.

Quilt Poem

Mahealani's hands
know quilting easy as freedom.
Push the needle,
tug the thread.
Push.
Tug.

Mahealani learned this art
from her mother and grandmother
who had learned it from
missionary women who came
to Hawai'i from New England.
Those pious ladies had no idea
Hawaiian women were already
masters of fabric.

Mahealani's grandmother would make
tapa, Hawaiian bark cloth, by pounding
the pulp of the mulberry tree
into sheets used for clothing and bedding.

Like so many other Hawaiian women
she knew the skill of dye and prints, adding her own personal touch.

Mahealani continues this tradition by
quilting for those rare nights
when the island's temperature dips below 70 degrees.
She makes designs based on local flora,
bright colours, ocean views or patriotism.

Her masterpiece is always on her bed.
This quilt shows deftness of skill and
attention to the different changes around her.

Her masterpiece is a quilt whose borders
consist of four Hawaiian flags.
In the mast corner, the Union Jack.
Then, eight stripes of white, red and blue
for each of the major islands.

When you look down at Mahealani's bed
you see the flags flying upside down
the international signal for a country in distress.
On the white centre field of the quilt
the crest of her Nation has been embroidered with diligence, absolute care.

Enclosing in on the crest are four white stars,
symbol of a foreign nation,
their edges sharpened by manifest destiny.

At night Mahealani snuggles herself beneath her quilt.
She looks down at the flag opposite her head, sees it flying as it should:
Unbound, not dominated by unwelcome alliances.

During the day Mahealani's hands
know quilting and resistance easy as freedom.
Push the needle,
tug the thread.
Push.
Tug.

KEALOHA

Kealoha is the founder of HawaiiSlam, Youth Speaks Hawai'i (twice international champions) and First Thursdays (the largest registered poetry slam in the world). Kealoha was featured on HBO's *Brave New Voices* series presented by Russell Simmons. He has featured at major venues throughout the world, including the Schiffbau (Zurich, Switzerland), the Bienal do Ibirapuera (São Paulo, Brazil) and the 2007 NFL Pro Bowl half-time show. He is the poetic vocalist for Henry Kapono's *Wild Hawaiian* project (nominated for a Grammy), and has served as Hawai'i's SlamMaster since 2003. Kealoha graduated with honors from MIT with a degree in nuclear physics, served as a business consultant in San Francisco and played around as a surf instructor prior to becoming a professional poet. Visit www.KealohaPoetry.com for more information.

Recess

Remember the days when we used to play
On the playground every day?

What was that thing we took?
Recess!!
Yeah that's right, recess . . .
15 minutes of sheer madness

15 minutes of running around
Getting down with all of your friends until the bell sounded
That inevitable bell
That wrought the well of time dry
And I
Remember those times so vividly
Licking Jell-O instant pudding
Off of our hands
Making forts out of sand
And doing everything you can to just play

When's the last time you took 15 minutes out of your day
To just run around and play?

We used to do this every day
It was a staple of our existence
And those days are now dissonant
But if you close your eyes you can remember it those 15 minutes that now seem trivial
But when you were a kid 15 minutes was ephemeral everlasting
It was a fleeting moment
But it was so freaking real

15 minutes was enough time to swing your brains out
Make a movie out of clouds
It was enough to climb in and out and around the monkey bars 5 times
It was enough time to join a game of 4 squares and make it up to king
Or fling red rubber spheres at each other in a game of dodgeball with 3 teams
       weaving in and out of rotation
It was enough for 2 friends to run up and down hills holding hands singing ridiculous bits
It was enough time to get 1 kick in a game of kickball
       and really that's all you ever needed was one kick to show everybody what's up
       and I never had the power to crank it long like Andrew Leong
       over the fence
       hence a home run
       but I could always get on base and tease
       my opposition into going for a squeeze play
       and I would escape easily
       obtaining that extra base
       with a facial disgracial, right?

When's the last time you grabbed your friends and played a game of kickball?
When's the last time you approached someone eating raw ramen
all crushed up inside the bag with the powder sprinkled all over it,
stuck out your hand and said those two magic words . . . 'I like'

When's the last time you just called someone and said 'let's ride bikes'
When's the last time you grabbed a carrot when you were in your bibadeez
     and sang into it like a mic
     not an 'MIC steady rhyming to the beats
     keeping yo' heads bobbing cuz my styles is deep'
     but I'm talking about grabbing a freaking carrot
     and singing some Lionel Richie or some bit like that . . .
     'All night long! All night!
     All night long! All night!
     Tom bo li de say de moi ya . . . hey Jambo Jumbo . . .'

We didn't even know what that stuff meant
But it sounded brilliant
The equivalent of Mozart in our modern day
It captivated the imaginations of our youth
And now I get obtuse stares when I be singing at the top of my lungs while driving alone . . .
People hear me out
Why are we striving so hard to grow up?

Why do we now in our free time call each other to go out and eat?
When did sitting down at a restaurant and eating a meal ever replace
creativity and the expression of the free spirit?
That stuff is so sterile to me
And I don't deal well with sterility
When did going out to dinner ever become an activity?
Sitting across the table from your friends and family
Breeds familiarity
But this type of formality is just too plain for me can't you see
Remember how it used to be?

The fantasies that speed through my brain
Are entertained by visions from long ago when we used to potluck on the beach
Yeah we'd eat, but then we'd teach each other how to flip, slide, ride, or fly
We could have done anything
It didn't matter it was engaging
It was entertaining
We were learning how to be active and creative together

Remember?

And now I see
The masses of our generations falling
Into the trap of daily routine
That unceasing monotony plaguing our society

And I be
Resisting
You see I don't deal well with monotony
When did watching TV ever become an activity?
Letting time pass performing passive viewing
Watching someone else do something we're not actually doing

Recessing through the eyes of someone else's 15 minutes of fame
When we could be out living our own 15 minutes of game . . .

Remember the days when we used to play
On the playground every day?

What was that thing we took?

Recess . . .

NINA KIRIFI-ALAI

Nina was born in Iva, Savai'i, Sāmoa, and grew up in Apia. Her father comes
from Iva and her mother is from Puapua, Vaimoso and Malie. Nina has a BA in
women's studies and an LLB from the University of Auckland and is currently
working as the manager of the Pacific Islands Centre at the University of Otago, a
post she has held since 2002. She also holds the high chief title of Tofilau from her
village of Iva. She is passionate about all things Pacific.

Alapati

He's small
Not too tall
Yet,
a very tall man
His hair a frizzy ball of black curls
crowned by time and wisdom with sina

Outlining his 'lulu' eyes
That could see into your soul
That could touch your conscience and discipline you on the spot
That could speak to your heart, reminding you who you are
O le tamāli'i
a very 'paū' man
with his leo pa'ulua
Revered by his colleagues
Respected by his people
Feared by the talavou
Or even misunderstood
As . . . too distant, or maybe too mamalu to be bothered by some wannabes
He's quiet
E tumu i le fa'aaloalo
But you can hear him from the Vaipē, Vaito'elau and the Vaimauga
Just a small man
Not too tall
But very loud.
'E kelē le kamāloa'

ANN MARIE NĀLANI KIRK

Ann Marie Nālani Kirk is an award-winning film-maker from Maunalua on the island O'ahu. She received her Masters degree from the University of Hawai'i Center for Pacific Islands Studies in Digital Storytelling.

The Market

The dirty black-footed girl
ran into the sleepy market
Her wind-blown hair
full of irritating knots
dropped into her eyes
She stopped in front of

the endless rows
of pregnant glass jars
and she read the words slowly
the magic words

    Li Hing Mui
    Baby Seed
    Shredded Mango
    Sweet Whole Seed
    Rock Salt Plum

From behind the cluttered counter
full of penny candies, marbles
and Pepto-Bismol
rose a tired voice,
'What you like, baby?'
The girl brushed the dark cloud
of hair from her eyes
'I like quarter's worth mango seed, Mamasan'

The crinkled blue woman
walked down the dusty aisle
with a small wooden shovel in her hand
She dug deep inside the belly of the mango seed jar
and weighed the contents on a rusty scale
Then placed the mango seed
in a tiny fresh-smelling brown paper bag
'Here you go, baby'
The girl reached down
the cotton cave of her shorts
and pulled out a sweaty 1972 quarter
finding a place for it on the jumbled counter
'Thanks, eh'

The girl opened the magical bag
and stuck her fingers in the gooey mess
she pulled out a long tan chubby piece of mango seed
She popped it into her impatient mouth
and ran out the market door

VICTORIA KNEUBUHL

Victoria Nalani Kneubuhl is of Hawaiian/Sāmoan ancestry and raised in both Hawai'i and American Sāmoa. She is a Honolulu playwright and author. Her plays have been produced in Hawai'i and the continental United States, and have toured to Britain, Asia and the Pacific. Her anthology, *Hawai'i Nei: Island Plays*, and her mystery novel, *Murder Casts a Shadow*, were published by the University of Hawai'i Press. In 1994, she received the prestigious Hawai'i Award for Literature and, in 2006, the Elliot Cades Award for Literature.

For Tasi (Dotsy)

We perform our last rites in
this circle of stones
built by our grandmother
all around she
planted these trees
that are not from here whose
perfumed flowers we have named
and now include in
all of our rituals today
we bury our beloved
aunt not of our blood family
by marriage a papālagi
born to the islands with
no other place
she called home.

This is not
a pre-packaged funeral
family digs her grave
family bathes and dresses
her body
writes her life
in one hundred words
or less
raises a tent
sets up chairs while

my sister and I
swelter in the heat
with pelu and clippers
wrenching flower
after flower from the bush
in the middle of the day
you shouldn't work like this
my father scolds
and I'm so grateful
it's not him
I'm doing this for.

Then comes the day
and the last time
we take her home in
a thread of black cars
winding along the sea
today it shines and rolls
Faga'alu, Fatu ma Futi, Matu'u
inland past Nu'uuli I
struggle for the names
of villages I used
to know them all then
finally up the long drive
to the circle of stones where
all of the āiga is waiting.

I try but cannot hear the man
in the black lavalava
who never knew her
his mumbling phrases from
the Bible fading
behind me is
the place her house
once stood the soil that
folded over her hands
year after year as
she fashioned an
enviable garden
from the impossible bush a
coconut tree where
she trained her
vanilla to climb and bloom
she showed me the

delicate process of pollination
all by hand she said
we make our lives.

So now I am waiting
and look above
for annunciation
I am looking
toward seamless
sky trees robed with
vines and falling flowers
when one by one they
arrive: the sega, the
ti'otala, the scruffy mynah
even our white
lulu turns up
for this day a
host of wings descending
to the circle
they stand sharp
eyed and ready
claws on branches
a single pua
twirls toward earth as
the voice of the 'iao
cries out the eulogy
she would
have loved.

Olo

On this ground the rocks flew
And the spears stabbed
At the blood flushing out
Heads were split by clubs
Cracking bones
Their cries at night
Sometimes you can hear them
For the ones they saw
Right before
They were cut off from
Those bodies sweating

Out the killing death
Forever
See those mounds
Raised fortifications
They are the evidence now
They tell us who sleeps underneath
This part of the earth
This ground
Our family calls
Home.

Over the bones and sites of war
They built the houses
Where we listened as our father told
How it was before the roads and
The lights and in the villages
Where he walked in the high valleys when
Every man had a tatau
Or he sat with the women he said
The vao had so many voices
You never hear them now
And how he could swim
Across the bay it was so clear
All the way he saw his shadow on the bottom
Then our mother would kiss us goodnight
In our beds veiled in mosquito nets
As the light went out
I could see them dancing
The old ones when
The moon came full across the yard
This place didn't need a
Sign that said
'Ua Sā.

From this theatre of war my uncle
Coaxed up the green things which
Flowering called back the birds
To where he wrote
All those words that still
Make us weep and cry
And long for each other
Then sometimes he would
Fight with my aunt
Who said that divisions

Should be official
So she madly paced and counted
And drew out all the boundary lines
I swear it was them down there
Our subterranean neighbours
They don't wonder why
We all look haunted
They don't wonder why
We have trouble getting along.

And then there was the time
My family brought me home
They thought it was to die
At twenty-two
Sick from the world all ready
With the taste of funereal dirt
In the back of my mouth my
Blood prepared me for burial
And I was more than willing
To give myself up
I was more than willing
To fall on this ground.

But in the fever dream
They all came calling
A formal visit
With feather-edged
Fine mats like flags
They sailed up the lawn
All the hundreds shining
They came up shining
Each one to embrace me
Each one with warrior arms
Each one bearing a meaalofa
Of love they came
Oiled
Scented
And finely dressed
For battle.

KAPULANI LANDGRAF

Born and raised in Pūʻahuʻula, Kāneʻohe, Kapulani Landgraf received her BA in anthropology from the University of Hawaiʻi at Mānoa and her MFA in photography from Vermont College. Landgraf's books *Nā Wahi Pana o Koʻolau Poko* and *Nā Wahi Kapu o Maui* gained Ka Palapala Poʻokela Awards for Excellence in Illustrative Books in 1995 and 2004. She currently teaches photography and Hawaiian visual art and design at Kapiʻolani Community College, Honolulu, Hawaiʻi.

Makaʻawaʻawa

White Woman

SUSANA LEI'ATAUA

Born in Wellington, New Zealand Susana Lei'ataua is from generations of orators and storytellers. She is part of the Lei'ataua and Taupa'u families of Manono, Sāmoa, and her mother's family has been in the Pacific for more than 150 years, sailing from England, Ireland and Scotland. She received the Fulbright New Zealand Senior Scholar Award in 2008, and was Artist-in-Residence at the Asian/Pacific/American Institute of New York University from 2007 to 2009.

Late Night Farewell

Bleary-eyed words
formulate themselves
in haste for your
fast moving page
'Be Thou my Vision,
O Lord of my heart;
Naught be all else to me,
save that Thou art.'
And they stand to sing
these thoughts like
voices of old
shaky with their need
to hit the notes
finding them first
before landing the Voice
and letting it ring out
'And did those feet in ancient time
Walk upon England's mountain green?'
Remains to be seen
but yours is the bird's
eye on the periphery and
mine also
and whether we feel bound
earthbound
or not
doesn't actually
necessarily

have anything to do
with flying.
Let us remind our wings
that travel is destination
focused and scheduled
as such;
flight is freedom
from such constraints
and the doing of the same
as imperative as breathing
and our 'how' 'where'
and 'why'
you are who you are
I am who I am
we are who we are.
I love you and celebrate
the pending height:
Go forth
Go there . . .
the stretch
the lift
the span
the horizon.

NAOMI LOSCH

Born in Kahuku, Oʻahu, Hawaiʻi in 1945, Naomi Losch, received her early education in the sugar plantation community on rural Oʻahu. She is of Hawaiian, Tahitian, Chinese and haole extraction and graduated from the Kamehameha School for Girls in Honolulu, a school for children of Hawaiian ancestry. She received her BA in anthropology and MA in Pacific Islands studies from the University of Hawaiʻi at Mānoa and is currently an associate professor of Hawaiian language at UHM. Naomi has taught Hawaiian language and culture at university level for nearly forty years.

Blood Quantum 2

Wat? You Hawaiian, you no look like! How much Hawaiian you?
One sixteent'?! Ho bra, so little bit, whea stay? In yaw small toe?
I tree quata, yeah, and we live homestead, too.
You no can, heh? You no mo' nuff blood.
Wat? Moʻokū . . . wat? Wat is dat? Genealogy?
Oh, I dunno dat kine stuff, my mudda she know.
How you know dat kine stuff? Yaw mudda went teach you?
You can talk Hawaiian? Wow, I no can, but I get the blood.
My mudda no can talk Hawaiian. I tink her grandmudda could.
Dey wen use Hawaiian when dey like talk stink about my mudda dem.
Wow, you can talk stink about us too now.
Ho, even if you get little bit Hawaiian blood, jes' like you mo' Hawaiian.
Cause you know Hawaiian kine stuff and can talk Hawaiian.
You sound jes' like my grandfadda but you no look like.
No can tell who is Hawaiian now days, yeah?

LUFI A. MATĀ'AFA LUTERU

Lufi A. Luteru traces her rich genealogy of Matā'afa to Salamumu, Saleaula, Asau and Satapuala, Sāmoa, spanning across wondrous Moananuiākea joining her maternal line to the Kanialama and Kahanu 'ohana of Kaua'i to the grand genealogy of 'Umialīloa of Hawai'i Island, linking back to Tahiti. A proud single parent, 'Ōiwi artisan, weaver, teacher and humble kama'āina of Mākaha Valley, she is currently in her last year of her Masters studies at Kamakakūokalani Center for Hawaiian Studies, Hawai'inuiākea School of Hawaiian Knowledge, at the University of Hawai'i at Mānoa, O'ahu.

Hi'uwai

ke one hānau
e ku'u kupunahine
I stand before you
in humbleness
witness to
the beauty of
wana'ao
lā'aukūlua moon
faintly   visible
        between
ka pō a me ke ao
cleanse me
mai ke po'o
a ke kapua'i
carry this gentle vessel
across ka Pākīpika
Te Moana Nui a Kiwa
grant the knowledge
and wisdom
waiting for
kupaianaha child
immersed in peace
I seek and receive
rejuvenation

Kukui

mana-ful seed
ka ulu lā'au
nā kini o ka 'āina
mālipolipo
    ancestral light
ignite   the roaring fire
deep   deep inside
na'auao   o ka pō
ka pouli   ka moauli
    beautiful soot
travel to the depths of
my sacred   mo'o'ōlelo
    penetrate
pores and kino lau
Godly bodies
hā   uliuli
our continuum
blackened is the mo'o
who seeks to speak
living   breathing
skin histories

BRANDY NĀLANI McDOUGALL

Brandy Nālani McDougall is a poet of Kanaka Maoli, Chinese and Scottish descent, born and raised in upcountry Maui. A 1994 graduate of the Kamehameha Schools, she received her Master of Fine Arts from the University of Oregon in 2001 and completed a Fulbright Award to Aotearoa New Zealand in 2002. She is the co-founder and chief editor of Kahuaomānoa Press and is working toward completing her PhD in English at the University of Hawaiʻi at Mānoa. Her dissertation focuses on contemporary Kanaka Maoli literature. Her first collection of poetry, *The Salt-Wind: Ka Makani Paʻakai*, was published by Kuleana ʻŌiwi Press in December 2008.

Waiting for the Sunrise at Haleakalā

Still half asleep, I drive toward the summit
and find a rhythm turning sharp corners,
leaning with each familiar curve. Outside,
the dark forms of abandoned ʻahu,
built by some ancestral hand, and high crowns
of silversword stand solemnly in black.
Above them, stars dim, slow as the rented
cars ahead, an uneasy Hertz convoy.
I curse them silently, knowing this road
and the view down of Maui, the muted
flickering of an island city's lights –
what distracts the rustle of tourist maps.
The fog filters our headlights, as our cars,
imposing on the calm, find their spaces.
In the unlit cold, a voiceless wind waits
for our doors to open, heaters to stop.
I carry blankets up the gazer trail
to the crater's edge and sit, staring down
a mouth full of blue clouds, a restless tide
covering, then clearing over the black.

Sitting here, above the clouds, I wonder
why I came, what led me to this sacred
place, expecting that it could awaken

the lost beginnings of my blood-answer
my dream of lava touching ocean, belts of steam
blown by the wind, green shoots of fern through rock.
Waking from this dream tonight, cold, restless,
afraid of forgetting where I came from,
I knew only to climb higher, to reach
the summit before sunrise, as Māui-
a-ka-malo did long ago. Lying here
against the cinder, he waited to snare
the sun, its sixteen hurried rays, with reins
of olonā. And I feel the same need
to slow the days, in their constant sway
of golf courses over graves and hotels
over heiau. Each hour soars as quick
as the jets above this child-shaped island
lost in traffic on the highways, the wind-
driven canefields burnt long into the night –
from Pukalani to Kīhei, Kula
to Lāhaina – no rest for paradise.

I close my eyes to listen to the air,
hoping to hear the ancient chants of hā
upwelling from the valleys, the still breath
of life, the inviolate sigh of love
I know lives in iwi beneath me, in rocks
born in the crater, lying where they fell.
But I hear nothing in the wind and clouds,
as the sky turns from black to blue, singing
a silent aubade to the swallowed stars,
to Maui, fading slowly with the moon.
Then, as the sun begins to stretch its rays,
lighting my tears, I remember how words
cannot hold such love flooding the valleys,
the aloha in pink roselani
buds blooming wild, full of new mountain rain.

Below, the clouds thin, and the crater floor
awakens, enrobed in red and gold cinder,
flush of colour woven into the earth.
And the tourists applaud the performance
before walking to their cars, turning back
for one last look at the sun in its house,
another camera's bright flash. But I stay,
easing off the blanket from my shoulders,

under a sun so close, I could touch it.
And I am grateful for the quiet lull,
for the time to sit among the scattered
grass, the silversword reaching for the sky –
and one lets me watch, opening its fire
in five hundred red flowers, each a sun
offering light from Haleakalā.

By the Blur of My Hands

> A standoff at Nanakuli Beach Park ended today with the loss of a
> man's life. After sitting in the stolen car with a gun for six hours, the
> man, identified by police as 25-year-old David Kalahiki, ran from
> police toward the water where he took his own life. Kalahiki has
> spent most of his 20s in prison for burglary and assault convictions.
> – Hawai'i News Register

The black asphalt creases the dry hillside,
sends up its heat in flares, warping the air
around me into a raw kind of fire.
And I stare at it through the cracked windshield
of this beat-up shit of a car I stole
because I knew there was no going back.
They'll find the dead man and know I killed him.
And soon, they'll find me here, their lights whirling
mad and their guns pointing back at my own.

With the ocean in the rear-view, I can't
help but cry into the wheel, hard, broken
tears for my hands, what they will never hold.
I tried, despite their useless stuttering,
their blur of deformed fingers, ugly stubs,
to make myself right, no matter. Even
drawing was too hard, colours crashed, red on
blue, over the paper and on the desk,
then the teacher's glare, whispers behind me.

I did what I could, waited twenty years
before letting my hands touch a woman
in the dark, where she wouldn't see my hands
plunge deep into her skirt, trembling as when
I washed dishes at the Red Dragon, cups
and plates breaking into shards as they fell

from my hands, like the dealer man last night,
chest open, so much blood where the bullet
tore his last breath, killed him and his money.

I cry for him now, knowing the mistakes
of my hands, that they can't blur his blood, nor
my own by this ocean, the same I fished
as a child, the cordage secure, for once,
in my grip. The waves washing salt over
rocks, the quiet glide of my hands guiding
the net in. And the pull outward after
each break, offering love more than mercy,
a faint whisper, *This is where you belong.*

On Finding My Father's First Essay, San Joaquin Delta College, 1987

It must have been hard for him on days
when the sun hit the muddy delta,
sending up what smelled like failure,
rotten and man-made. Still, he drove
his old, rusty car down Pacific to
the college, where he sat by those
half his age who knew little of how
they would begin, how easily beginnings
turn into a thousand dark miles of water.
But they knew school, much more about it
than he did – which words to use when,
how to give nothing but the requirement,
to hide between clauses and commas.
This was his mistake of the essay
called 'What Life Means to Me':

> *My shadow on the ocean's face, the frayed*
> *water behind a boat. Rainbows and valleys*
> *and leis for my daughters, that they forgive*
> *me for leaving and all that I couldn't give.*

Some nameless face read through it, asking
for predicates, circling fragments, then went on,
knowing our father's tears, yet deeming them
unremarkable. I can see his hands thumbing
the red-marked page, searching for a glimpse

of understanding and finding none, his face
burning with shame for not knowing how much
it would take to begin again, to go back across
the water. He must have left that day thinking
he had to work even harder for our love, to be
a real father, responsible and clean as grammar.

On Cooking Captain Cook

If you ask the blonde-haired concierge
at the Grand Kīhei, he will tell you
that we ate him whole,
>strung his white meat on a stick,
>filled his mouth with apples,
>and slow-roasted him over fire.

The sunburned vendor selling t-shirts
in Lāhaina will say we ate him, too,
but only certain parts:
>the head, heart, hands
>wrapped in a kind of spinach
>and held over hot lava.

The owner of the Hoola-Hoola Bar
and Grill will say we only ate him
for lack of fine cuisine,
>rubbed his skin with sea salt
>then boiled him in coconut milk
>and served him on a bed of yams.

My anthropology professor, long researching
ancient cultures, will offer explanations
from his latest book:
>The white-skinned men seemed gods
>to those without metal or written words.
>By eating him they meant to become him.

But if you ask my tūtū
while she waters her orchids and protea
she will invite you in
to eat, to eat.

Kukui

'ekahi

You hold within your heart
enough to fire-stir the night,
along with the possibility
of inamona, the sweet roasting
of your meat in communion
with the pa'akai – a delicate
offering of heat, light and a full 'ōpū
of properly seasoned poke.

I know you by your gifts.

'elua

Today, I sat under your tangled canopy
of branches and leaned against you,
the shallow ridges of your trunk's bark
against my cheek. Bright bursts
of clouded sky were being reshaped
by your leaves stroking the wind.

Yours is a subtle, unbending hula
timed by the uneven beat of your many
hard-shelled nuts falling against
the grass, and I thought mostly of how easy
it could be to let go of words like that,
to harvest the dark-shelled secrets
that have bent me under their weight.

Haumea

Out of her head,
Out of her breast,
Out of her mouth,
Out of her eyes,
Out of her skin,
Out of her breath,

Came the gods who lived
off the length of her body,
offering their piko in return,

Came the soft green curve
of the sun falling into the ocean,

Came the encrusted salt pans,
the cooled fields of pāhoehoe and ʻaʻā,

Came the first young fern shoots
over the insects who work
unseen and unheard,

Came the stars strewn as seeds
in the heavens, spread by her hands
and sown across the dark soil of space,

Come the offshoots of those long-germinated seeds.

DAN TAULAPAPA McMULLIN

Dan Taulapapa McMullin is a painter and poet. His paintings and sculpture have been exhibited at Okaioceanikarts Gallery, McCarthy Art Gallery and Fresh Gallery Ōtara in Aotearoa, as well as the Bishop Museum in Honolulu, the Gorman Museum at University of California, Davis, and with the Indigenous Forum at the United Nations. He won a Poets&Writers Award from The Writers Loft in Saint Paul, and a Best Short Film Award from the Rainbow Film Festival of Honolulu. His parents, Lupelele and Samuelu, are from Manu'a and Tutuila in American Sāmoa. He is teaching a course on the contemporary art of Oceania at the University of California, Irvine, but his heart is always in Sāmoa.

A Ghost

In Lagituavalu a ghost roamed the land,
it was a crying ghost and it lived in the trees.
People talked about the crying ghost and what a nuisance it was.
They petitioned the Governor to do something,
send it away on priority mail, or maybe express mail post haste.

The workers at the airport told the workers at the post office.
The workers at the post office told the fire department.
The fire department told the police.
The police chief visited the attorney general.
The attorney general called his sister the governor's wife.
The governor's wife said to her husband in bed that night, 'Call the president.'
The governor's wife's husband said,
'No . . . Let God solve things in his own time . . .'

But God let it all go,
because the ghost was on a sacred journey through Lagituavalu.
'Life is a dream, nothing comes to sleepers but a dream,'
as the song went on the radio, over and over,
'Far beyond the sky, the source of everything.'

Every time the song came on again, the ghost began wailing, wailing,
until the governor's wife called the radio station herself and asked,
'Please, please stop playing that song, I can't stand it any more.'

But the radio station attendant replied,
'I can't do anything about it,
the DJ went to Lagituafitu to attend a conference,
everything you hear is on a tape
and I can't stop it because it's looped.'

After a very long time
when people began getting used to the wailing of the ghost
and even little children would no longer wake up and notice it crying in the night,
God, walking about came upon a talie tree with big waxy leaves
and hearing the tired ghost snoring through the wood, told it,
'My dear, the one you seek is not here.'

Waking, the ghost shook itself from the tree's trunk and branches
pouring like rain from the leaves, and rising like mist from the grass
it went away at last from Lagituavalu, the Eighth Heaven,
back to Lalolagi, the Earth,
back to the land of the living.
For the crying ghost was a living person in Lagituavalu the land of the dead
where the living are only ghosts, and the real ghosts are flesh and blood.

And back in Lalolagi the land of the living
I broke a glass again, against the kitchen sink.

Jerry, Sheree, and the Eel

Jerry always stayed in the kitchen
that's what fags in American Sāmoa do
take care of the young
the old, haunt the kitchen, cooking
and washing dishes. Anyway,
one usually saw Jerry
at the kitchen sink.

Now, this part of the story I made up:
One day
a missionary gave Jerry an eel to cook
but Jerry knew it was a sacred eel
and was taken by it.
He kept it in a rain barrel filled with water
as a pet. A sacred pet.

This other part's real again:
Every once in a while
Jerry put on a bright frock
beat her face and caught a taxi to town.
Pago Pago!

As Sheree she went to all the clubs
and asked all the straight boys to dance
because she only danced with straight boys.
And of course they all did
because you know
it's impolite to a person's entire family
to say, No.

Meanwhile
the sacred eel
grew larger and larger,
until its head was the size of a coconut.
Sheree, screaming,
made a pond to hold it.

This part's true:
One day
Sheree decided to form her own club with all the fa'afafine on the island.
They called themselves the Daughters of Sāmoa.
Sheree grew her hair long,
dyed it red
and got a job as Executive Secretary to the President of American Sāmoa Community
College,
which she runs to this day.

And the ending I made up:
One night
the sacred eel grew so large
(as tall as a coconut tree)
that it chased Sheree
from village
to village
through
all
of
Sā
Moa.

OLE MAIAVA

Ole Maiava is a proud father of three. An independent film-maker, actor, broadcaster, musician, published poet, visual artist and short-story writer, he is also a member of the Banana Boat writers' group. He is currently the director of the Pasifika Festival in Auckland, New Zealand.

Filemu Sāmoa!

Strip my skin, pull it bare,
Pluck my eyebrows, colour my hair,
Drill my teeth, knock them straight,
Change my walk, shorten my gait,
Dress me down, break my smile,
Droop my shoulders, depress my style,
Fix my stare, cover the pain,
Loose my mana, make me insane,
Kill me with Spanish Flu,
Twenty thousand dead, what do you do,
Send the troops, shoot me down,
Shed our blood, hide our frown,
Tamasese is no more,
Filemu, filemu Sāmoa,
Hear them cry, hear them scream,
Ua uma le Mau, shatters the dream,
Sāmoa mo Sāmoa is the chant,
Rule New Zealand but you can't,
The natives are there to be used,
Maltreated and abused,
Rule New Zealand by oppression, independence gained through loss and depression,
Bungling administration, laws of immigration,
New Zealanders killed twenty thousand lives, children, husbands and wives,
So come to New Zealand to fulfil a dream,
Which still echoes with the scream, Filemu Sāmoa!

SELINA TUSITALA MARSH

Selina Tusitala Marsh is of Sāmoan, Tuvalu, English and French descent. She was the first Pacific Islander to graduate with a PhD in English from the University of Auckland and is now a lecturer in the English Department, specialising in Pacific literature. Marsh is the co-ordinator of Pasifika Poetry (www.nzepc.auckland.ac. nz/pasifika) – a sister site of the New Zealand Electronic Poetry Centre. She is the author of *Fast Talking PI* (AUP, 2009), editor of *Niu Voices: Contemporary Pacific Fiction 1* (2006) and is currently working on a critical anthology of first-wave Pacific women poets writing in English. Her academic and creative writing deal with issues that affect Pasifika communities in Aotearoa New Zealand and indigenous peoples elsewhere. She lives on Waiheke Island with her family.

Cardboard Crowns

morning

I'm with
eighteen year olds
we talk about the crisis
in NZ lit
and the problem of reading
like
they don't

there's a fictional yawn from the back

their books weigh down
their bodies not their minds

afternoon

I'm cooking with five year olds
sculpt flour, yeast, water
mozzarella fingers dip and rise

I keep an eye
on my new starter

his bony body
under an over-confident uniform

he's educating me
in bravery

yesterday

I'm baking a cake and roasting a chicken
simultaneously

blowing up gold balloons
taping them to the king's throne
a creased kindy hat becomes a tama āiga crown
as green spears fan between toetoe heads
over a crayoned five

kids said the chicken was good
it tasted like cake

today

the eighteen year olds buzz over
Wendt's 'Robocop in Long Bay'
theory pop pops the air
V guarana cans
moor the tables
as the book floats away

I throw out a life line
but no one's read it

tomorrow

the five year olds
are Tagaloa's boat builders

o le tala i tufuga o le vaa o Tagaloa

they stomp-sing, pull
fell and gnaw with their teeth in the dark
till they see the dawn

they know when to hide
they've all read the story

A Sāmoan Star-chant for Matariki

fetu tasi

I call forth Mata Ariki, the Eyes of God
to watch over Papatūānuku and her people
I call forth wishes for the new June moon
spoken in shadow corners
steaming in palmy places

fetu lua

I call forth the pickled eel in brine
lolling like tongues of story
let loose under a feasting sky
I call forth the moki and korokoro
to fatten nets
that they might feel the weight
of wealth in giving

fetu tolu

I call forth matariki ahunga nui
the overturning of the earth
the bearing of new seedlings
I call forth the kūmara and kalo
rooting in fanua for this divine moment
of cyclic beginnings
I call forth the planting of all things
fresh in the soil of the mind

fetu fa

I call forth the pākau
the six-tailed kites
to tickle the heavens
make us laugh
I call forth kete bulging with treasures
woven histories pressed
and plaited by kuia thumb

fetu lima

I call forth the smaller hand
unfurling in the bigger
whānau spiralling like
an unfathomable prime
I call forth the harvesting of whakapapa
the sowing of blood lines
the clearing of weeds from graves
the tihei in that first born breath

fetu ono

I call forth the knotting of star-charts
by sinnet and shell
I call forth the vaka and all manner of vehicle
navigating by our light
into the long safe journey home
into the uncharted night

fetu fitu

I call forth the rising of my six sisters
in Ranginui's pre-dawn cloak
I call in greeting
talofa mata ali'i
ia orana matarii'i
aloha makali'i
kia ora matariki
I call forth the music of bone flutes
the chant, the song, the karakia
guiding the traveller's feet
and heavenward eyes

Two Nudes on a Tahitian Beach, 1894

Gauguin,
you piss me
off.

You strip me bare
assed, turn me on my side
shove a fan in my hand
smearing fingers on thigh
pout my lips below an
almond eye and silhouette me
in smouldering ochre.

I move
just a little
in this putrid breeze
hair heavy to
fuscous knees, still
I'm the pulse
on the arm of this wall
and I've drawn her to me again.

Here she comes.

Not liking that she likes me
not liking you, but knowing that she
likes me, not liking you
liking me, but she
likes me and sees me,
but not you,
because you
Gauguin,
piss us
off.

JEAN MASON

Jean Tekura Chapman Mason was born in Rarotonga in the Cook Islands. Her mother is a Māori of Ma'uke and Atiu descent. Her father, who migrated from Britain as a child, was a naturalised New Zealander. Jean was educated in the Cook Islands and New Zealand. She is director of the Cook Islands Library and Museum Society. In 2000 Mason co-edited an edition of *Mana – Cook Islands Special*, an anthology of Cook Islands writing, and in 2001 she published *Tatau*, her first collection of poems. She has written a series of cultural articles for an anthology of Cook Islands writers called *Akono'anga Māori: Cook Islands Culture*, which was published by the Institute of Pacific Studies in 2003. Mason also writes documentary scripts for local productions and articles for *Escape*, a popular tourist magazine.

Turakina Street

i Uru Anthony (née Mouauri), a Ma'uke woman living in Grey Lynn, Auckland, 1964

I give you
these baskets and 'ei
made by my hands
in the old style
from plastic packing strips
my way of keeping alive those ties
to home
in this land not my own
there are no pandanus leaves here
but there are jobs for me and all my brothers and sisters
we will send you what we can
when we can
we catch buses every day
and we clock in every morning
the hours are long but the pay is good
you may cut the pandanus I planted as a girl
and we will exchange our crafts
when next we meet
my sister, my husband and I
and all our children

live at Turakina Street
we still make pai every Sunday
and share it with all the clan

ii Uru's daughter, Jacinta, 1985

Ma'uke follows me
like a shadow
to the new country
Mum took our son's afterbirth
and buried it under a tree
and he will have a life filled with good fortune
I listened to my mother
and saved my money
and married a good man
and we bought a brick and tile house in the suburbs
I have learned to cook island meals
and European ones too
I have a European education
so I don't have to work long hours
in a hot kitchen or laundry
we don't have open-house every Sunday
my husband and I share mum's values
we eat pai occasionally –
when we take the kids to mum's place
at Turakina Street

iii Uru's grandson (Jacinta's son), Ben, 1992

I have lots of friends at the school I go to
from all races and religions
I love playing with the children
and visiting Nana's
and playing with my cousins
and listening to the old women tell stories
about Ma'uke
My great-uncles tease me
and call me names in Ma'ukean
I eat all kinds of nice food at home
but I love pai at Nana's best of all
at Turakina Street

Teina

Always remembered him as old, square-jawed and gold-toothed, vain and smiling; lived in a little house with a Eurasian wife he didn't speak to for fifteen years. At the dinner table she sat rigid and silent while he ate.

He laboured in the sun in his youth – a handsome brown-skinned man. Watched Joe Louis flicks by night. He sang *Ou, ou, ou e, te vaine Anami*, in praise of Anamese women. Danced with his older brothers at Makatea, before a rail cart ran over him. Near death in a French hospital.

A miner. A Christian. A hypocrite. His back straight and strong at seventy-nine, unbent by years in phosphate mines. His dark eyes glistened like blackest pearls in his still unlined face. His wife and eldest daughter squabbled over his body the day he died in a French hospital.

Not that kind of Māori

At the Auckland Museum
An old Pākehā woman asks me
what the meaning of those patterns are
in the tukutuku panels on the walls of the whare
I'm sorry but I don't know
I'm not that kind of Māori
What kind of Māori are you, she asks
Cook Islands Māori
Never heard of them, she says.

Today, I have learned that there's a story in the red,
black and white patterns
This one is the southern night sky: that's the Southern Cross
These are Takurua and Puanga.

TRIXIE TE ARAMA MENZIES

Trixie Te Arama Menzies was born in Wellington in 1936 and lives in Auckland with her husband, Barry Menzies. She is of Tainui and Scottish descent. She has three adult children, five surviving grandchildren, four great-grandchildren and several mokopuna atawhai. She has taught at secondary schools, at the University of Auckland and been a kaiāwhina at kōhanga reo. Her four poetry collections are *Uenuku* (Waiata Koa, 1986), *Papakainga* (Waiata Koa, 1988), *Rerenga* (Waiata Koa, 1992) and *In the Presence of My Foes* (Waiata Koa, 2000). Together with Ramai Te Miha Hayward, the late Arapera Hineira Kaa Blank, Toi Te Rito Maihi and others, Trixie is a founding member of Waiata Koa, a Māori women's artists and writers collective that was formed at the time of the *Karanga* exhibition in 1986.

Once –

heading
home, we stopped
at Ōrewa, stayed in a motel
For once the kids weren't fighting
Maybe because we weren't –

In the morning we made coffee, looked outside
The tide was on the turn, just coming in

The water whispered as it gently broke
The sea was smoothed back to a golden line
The kids were down there playing on damp sand

He said, It's good, taking your family away,
Of course, it costs a bit of dough –
But his tone said that for once he didn't mind.

For once that time we seemed to get it right.

No Smoke without Fire

The young girl is running running she will not stop
Her lips are curled back, her eyes wide and staring,
     and her hair is tangled
She clutches her empty kit, sobbing and gasping
For her spilt pipis, fallen when she took flight
It was a hot blue day when she set out to gather them
With her ripening cousins, complete with togs and
     transistor
Giggling and gossiping. Smoking a little, illicitly
Their fire put out, the tide leaving the shore
They waded out to where the shells were plentiful
But she thought there might be more over the track
Jolly uncle turned up and went too, helping her over
That beach was deserted and uncle, seizing the
     moment
Showed his affection, engulfing her in his arms
Touched her under her clothes, gave her hard word,
     hard muscle
And his rough skin and stale hangover breath
He offers ten dollars, she is afraid of her mother
She heads for the river, her golden thighs flashing
     like flax blades
A rosy blush rising in her young skin like the dawn
He is after her, she is not going to embarrass him
His strong strides bring him closer until at the creek
She trips and falls, still clutching her kit with one pipi
Caught in the side, the last food of her girlhood
He is on her, he will prove once and for all who is
     master
He takes her into a cave under the earth
Slimy and sinful, starless night enters her being
The colours go out, she belongs to him now, she is
     death

Far behind them her mother is searching the beach
     for her daughter
Not wanting to face her suspicions she gropes for her matches
Lights her cigarette, and drags hard on her
     desperation

Ocean of Tongues

So many busy tongues, they are like an ocean
washing me this way and that, like a piece of seaweed –
Do your worst! I deny nothing
Whatever you can think up to say about me
I admit in advance –
I do not intend to argue
I am tossed about, clinging to bits of wreckage from
       my canoe
Hoping to rebuild it out of the broken ends
Would you think it justice if I drown?
Do not come to my rescue, the steering paddle has
       rotted
I would rather take my chance in the sea than be
       pierced by rot –
Rather, see to the paddle!
I will climb aboard the approaching ship that offers
       protection –
Meantime I remember my powerful ancestors and
       keep swimming

COURTNEY MEREDITH

Born in 1986, Courtney Meredith is an English graduate from the University of Auckland, where she co-edited *Spectrum 5*. Courtney has tutored poetry workshops for Tautai Contemporary Pacific Arts Trust, New Zealand Book Month, Ngāti Whātua, Corbans Estate Arts Centre and her own initiative for youth, Spread the Word. She has exhibited her poetry on vinyl and film with her collective, Forward Frangipani. She credits her late grandmother Rita Meleisea Meredith and her mother, Kim Meredith Melhuish, as the driving forces behind her writing.

No Motorbikes, No Golf

'Way South'

I said where you from baby? And you said

       Way South.

Nup
     nah

never been there
what grows there
women or moss?

And you said

      Way South flowers

purple hearts with blood grape trim and hymns
hymns like cotton fish across the white sun

a smoky cherub wide-eyed chorus
wailing on and calling on and falling on

hymns rise up from the baking tar
a rose cloud of voice

a crimson Cortina on the corner and Lorna is a nice name for a girl
and Paola is a nice name for a black Tahitian pearl

hymns rise up from the shadow limbs and yard milk sodden mouth
out the back round the back down the back and you said

Way South.

It isn't like an Island nipple nup
no breezing trees and caramel sand

no coconut truths spilling over woven fans
no plans of making love to the land.

There isn't a wooden face to stand my hands against and still
the rising falling chest, the salty dusky mess

Way South like a bat back to hell.

Babies grow in babies leaving paisley prints on ladies' skin
finer than and greener than a pounamu teardrop in the eyes of no man's land.

But can you hear the voices?
Clear as chimes at dusk

we eat sea hearts black and pulsing
skin the shells of silver rust

this is where the angels come
to down their wings and cuss

Te Henga caves make pilgrims brave
to shatter rock and bust

Way South like dead love walking wailing crawling

back to lust.

You can spy the timber spine of every creature on his step
straight for cemeteries resting heads and flower beds on top of death beds
joking 'bout the big smoke and the doubts that will not rest.

Souls pity the metal facts of the city
nodding that we've missed the dunes and cliffs

lining pebbles skyward, gift upon gift
the mountain body stands and lies

Way South

where the beast sleeps

Way South

with its mean streets
and ciggy-stained teeth.

Nup
    nah

never been there
what grows there?

'Mothers pray for sons
sons pray for brothers
fathers search for daughters
sisters wait for lovers

      Way South
        Way South'

Cloth saints

Dark boys high on the hill
are dead as the bright leaves falling

walking their bikes up the dusty track
stopping to smoke and look at the ants

like lost stars
set above the city
they pretend no one they love
is buried there.

KARLO MILA

Karlo Mila (Karlo Mila-Schaaf) is of Tongan and Pākehā descent. She was born in Aotearoa New Zealand, grew up in Palmerston North and has lived and worked in Auckland and Tonga. Her writing first appeared in *Whetu Moana*, and she has since had two books of poetry published by Huia Publishers, *Dream Fish Floating* (2005), which won the NZSA Jessie Mackay Award for best first book at the 2006 Montana New Zealand Book Awards, and *A Well Written Body* (2008). Karlo regularly performs poetry live and her poetry has been featured in a number of anthologies. She is currently completing her PhD, writing a regular op-ed column for the *Dominion Post* and working on her first novel. Karlo is married and has two young sons.

Visiting Tonga: A Sestina Variation

Pālangi you call me but I am not white
I don't know the words but I feel at peace within these walls
humming hymns in the church of Zion. I don't see
Sisu, no. But love?
Yes, I'm not just passing time
on a slow sluggish Sunday. Here where God is Love, I feel it too.

Sisu Kalaisi is always white.
And blond most of the time
on the cheap Taiwanese tapestries Tongans love
his fair haloed image hangs from church walls
and inside homes and on graves too,
blowing in the wind his blue eyes never seem to see . . .

The problem with Tonga is that it is just too
small, my cousin says to me. Even if you aren't walled
in (by brothers / mothers) there are eyes everywhere – and worse – mouths. See
they call this cousin of mine fie pālangi, 'wanting to be white',
with her notions of freedom she is ahead of her time.
She wants to marry for love.

An elderly aunt invites me into her fale, wallpapered in white
newspaper sheets of the *Tongan Times*
her house is an unintentional shrine to 8 May 1999, when the walls
were pasted anew and poverty – well read between the headlines love –
my aunt cannot tell you what happened on that day. See,
we see and we don't see too.

But then you don't need to know how to read in order to love
the King. An incident I chanced to see,
the King in a vaka, rowed by strong men, concentration fierce, keeping in time
wood ploughing through the water and at the walls
of the vaka swam a school of human fish, kicking up white
out of blue. Breathless but keeping up, wanting to honour their king too.

The palace is almond icing white
resting its creaking bones on a beach, cannon within its walls
this is blasted occasionally to prove a point. But see
love
of subjects is not the point most of the time.
The logic goes that a flatulent big bang commands respect (and fear too).

What am I but a Love child who seeks out an absent parent
　　　　　and mostly misunderstands. She sees
me too. Tonga whispers from within the walls
of a white shell: 'Koe ha mea fia ma'u? Lau pisi!
　　　　　Plenty time. No hurry. Ha'u kai' . . .

Virgin Loi

looking back,
do I wish I had a Tongan mother
who guarded my chastity
with a Bible in one hand
and a taufale in the other?
instead of my pale, polite pālangi mum
who gave me the freedom to choose
and understood that all the rest of the girls I knew
used tampons

do I wish I'd had a Tongan mother
who put the fear of God himself into me
so that in the heat of many moments

I'd say No
I'm worth more
let's see the rock
buy me shit
and treat me like a princess
(until after we're married
and then I'll be your baby making
black eyed doormat)

those Tongan girls
I see them stare
see my skin half pālangi fair
I watch your nostrils flare
I see you sio lalo

I know the coconut wireless
is so efficient
that I cannot get away
with what's actually true
let alone what is pure libel

once I thought I had a choice
and a right to choose
and I believed that ignorance
wasn't bliss
and experience
led to wisdom

I see you sio lalo

so what, I say
I won't wear white on my wedding day
cream suits me better anyway
I say
laughing on the outside
but on the inside
my hymen is broken

For Ida

first Pacific woman judge

Once I wrote

that we are the seeds of the migrant dream
the daughters supposed to fill the promise
hope heavy on our shoulders
we stand on the broken back of physical labour
knowing the new dawn has been raided.

But

we are the seeds of a much greater dream
that goes back across oceans of memory
a vision still held in the hands
of humble men buried in humble villages
who chant clear our paths
with every lost breath.

Ida, you have spoken of the sacrifice
of language lost, and the cost,
of success in the pālangi world
and you have wrapped your son safely
in fa'asāmoa
he rests in a nest of language
learning to tame words
that flew *like* wild gulls
far beyond our understanding.

'This is the sacrifice of my generation'
you said
'but it will not be his,
this is where the sacrifice stops.'

The gulls circle
and nest
and our sense of selves
rests.

You touch a vision
clasped to the breast
of humble women buried in humble villages
who still sing
across oceans of memory
in words that our children will be able to hear.

Eating Dark Chocolate and Watching Paul Holmes' Apology

i am sucking on a sante bar / sneaked / bought at pak'n'save
in a cigarette gold wrapper / i remember when you bought
them in dairies / they were stripped and served undressed /
edges worn from the friction / getting down with the
brown / chocolate dust was in the air

i am watching paul holmes apologise for calling kofi annan a
darkie / darkie takes me back to

6 years old / school grounds / see-saws / we won the
war / we won the war in 1944 / mean boys alternating
between catch and kissing and sticks and stones / darkie /
tania got called blackie / golliwog / i remember being
thankful i was pretty and fair / and had long hair / no one
called me manu off playschool or darkie / i was a milk
chocolate glass and a half / half caste / caramello enough to
be safe from bitter dark accusations

tonight paul holmes apologised for calling kofi annan a
darkie / takes me back to

10 years old / sitting on my dad's stomach / him flat on the
sofa / we're watching a week night movie / southern
drawls and white sheets / me crying hot wet tears over
black men with hurt in their eyes / what does lynching
mean maka? / my daddy / dark / my feet dangling off his
tummy / me *milky* brown chocolatey sweet / wanting
to grow up and be the prime minister / or a lawyer like
matlock / make everything all right for darkies everywhere

tonight paul holmes apologised for calling kofi annan a
darkie / takes me back

15 years old / barry / surf lifesaver / washboard abs /
the mattel man / automatic winking machine / ambivalent
crush / half hate / half fetish / blonde frosting in his fringe /
darkies / that's what he called us / hope you don't mind
darkies / he said / setting up his mate / flirting on the phone

tonight paul holmes apologised for calling kofi annan a
darkie / takes me back

17 years old / do you think they would ever let a boonga
be prime minister / corey p / dreadlocked bob marley
wannabe / says to me / mocking laughter / he's drunk at
three / in highbury / but we never dreamed they'd let an
indian woman be mayor of dunedin / so let's sukhi it to
them corey p / we were darkies anonymous then / making
fun of ourselves before anyone else could / revolution in
the bottom of a bong / cutting off our veins to spite our
lives /

tonight paul holmes apologised to the nation

i am 28 / aucklander / jokes about jaffas don't involve
māoris and minis / just another f-ing aucklander / the
p.i.'s here outnumber prejudice in wide open spaces /
skinheads low key / less closely shorn / too much rugby
league brawn / on the arms of coconuts / i've been told
i'm the cream rising to the top / the cream of the crop /
nesian queen / rank and file member of the chocolate
soldier movement / getting down with the brown /

tonight paul holmes apologised

sorry / he said / i've hurt my family / i may have hurt
yours /

yes / we scrapped in the car over it / there was yelling / by
the time we got to the end of the māngere motorway / i
was crying / who is this redneck with the big brown
shoulders sitting next me / anti pc / darker than me /
defending freedom of speech / but i don't want it to be all
right /

/ i don't want my kids to have stanzas of darkie memories /

sorry / paul holmes said / i could see that he meant it / i felt
sad for him / and happy / i signed the petition to say he
should get sacked / i am a manager in a govt department /
not matlock / not the pm / just a member of the chocolate
soldier movement / melting in the middle

Legendary

You are my Māui-tikitiki-a-Taranga
demigod to me
trickster of the heart
I just hope I'm pulling you in
because you could slow the sun for me
Māui
you could have
every finger of my fire
but remember
I am woman
and I do not doubt
that you will die
between my legs

MICHAEL O'LEARY

Born in Auckland, New Zealand, in 1950, Michael John O'Leary is of Irish and Te Arawa descent. He has a BA from Otago University and an MA from Victoria University of Wellington. He is at present completing a PhD at Victoria University on the status of women writers in New Zealand from 1945 to 1970. O'Leary is a writer, researcher and publisher, and currently lives in Paekākāriki. He has written articles, stories and book reviews for newspapers and journals, including the *New Zealand Listener* and the *Sunday Star-Times*. O'Leary has published more than thirty books of poetry, fiction and non-fiction, most recently *Alternative Small Press Publishing in New Zealand 1969 to 1999* (2008), the final instalment of his novel trilogy, *Magic Alex's Revenge* (2009), and, with David McGill, *G'Day Country Redux* (2009).

Livin' ina Aucklan'

all too soon it is over
stepping down on to the platform
(an almost perfect concrete curve of old-world technology)

and watching the train move away towards the west
like a memory of love

a railway is the most melancholy of transport modes
and when you are aboard
the motion is one of subtle love-making
– as the train pulls out
from the station you stepped down at . . .

it is your lover leaving, rolling down the track

all this on a two-minute trip to Avondale
but I defend the suburban services
saying romance is not confined to the Orient Express
and Mount Albert is as important as Montmartre
if you live there

once new and unknown
love is like a railway ticket held in my hand
but it has been clipped
as I stand alone on wind-swept Avondale platform
watching the train pull out of the station, I . . .

CHRISTY PASSION

Christy Passion was born and raised in Honolulu, Hawai'i. She began writing after college, in an attempt to find out more about her Hawaiian heritage. Her poetry and short stories have won numerous awards, including an Academy of American Poets Award, the James M. Vaughn Award for Poetry and the *Atlanta Review* International Merit Award. She has been featured in many journals and anthologies and released her first book, *No Choice but to Follow* (Bamboo Ridge Press), in April 2010.

Hear the Dogs Crying

A recording of her voice, an old woman's voice
full of gravel and lead steeped through
the car radio. She spoke of gathering limu
visitors on ships, and dusty roads in Wai'anae.
In the distance you could almost hear
the dogs crying, the mullet wriggling in the fish bag

Nostalgic for a tūtū I never knew,
I feel the ocean pulse inside me
waves rolling over, pushing me till I leap
from this car through the congested H-1
across the noise and ashen sky
emerge beneath the rains in Nu'uanu.
I move past the freshwater ponds
past the guava trees towards homes
with flimsy tin roofs where
my father, already late for school,
races up Papakōlea with a kite made
of fishing twine. Framed in a small kitchen
window, tūtū scrapes the meat from awa skin
for dinner tonight, wipes her hands on
old flour bags for dish cloths.
She is already small and wants to forget
I may be too late –

I have tomatoes and onion from the market, tūtū,
my hand is out, my plate is empty
and some bones for the dogs to stop their crying
do you know my name?
I am listening for your stories to call me in
my hand is out, my plate is empty
for your stories to show me the way
tūtū, do you know my name?

It Was Morning

on viewing Choris's portrait of Kamehameha I

It was morning when I first saw you
on a slim side wall where
someone might absentmindedly flip
a light switch. Not the centre of the gallery
with guards flanking you, cordoned off
by velvet ropes. Instead

you are housed in a small common frame
constricted by a fading red vest.
Your gray hair creates a halo effect;
a pious merchant, an ageing choirboy. Impostor.

Where are you, my king?

You are there, a shadow on the horizon
amidst a fleet of ten, a hundred, a thousand,
engulfing as the waves that surround this island,
seated on the ama, eyes perched on the shores of Waikīkī.
You are there in the tall grass of Nuʻuanu,
sun gleaming off your thighs, your chest.
Moʻo skin helmets your face allowing
only the black pupil widening to be seen,
your calloused hand holding back the spear
anxious for the release. You are there
in the first clashes of muscle and teeth,
salt sweat drawing light on to your skin
as the ʻelepaio shrieks in the branches above.
Your spear tip pushes father and brother to the edge
Imua! Imua! and 400 more leap like mullets
into stony nets waiting below.

A pact of silence has been made by the bones left behind,
I go to those pastures to break it. I go to listen
to find you, my king. Too many have been misled by this canvas.

Prepare to Move into the White House

I imagine you would take us with you,
perhaps rolled up in a Persian rug
or tucked in hidden pockets of your luggage
carrying white shirts, socks, and underwear.

There is no need to take us out
right away, no need to show us around.
Forget about us as you do your spine or spleen.

But when old chains begin to rattle
in your mind, or on the lips of suits
lining red carpeted hallways
that no longer seem new to you

we will be there; trade winds twisting
down the Ko'olau, fragrant fallen mangoes,
nests of salt. Let us offer you respite, let us
be a toehold in the craggy wall you climb
treading a new path to a new country.

Let us remind you of when hope
was measured in pocket change
after a long day of body surfing –
just enough for shaved ice and the bus ride home.

MAHEALANI PEREZ-WENDT

Mahealani Perez-Wendt is a Kanaka Maoli writer and political activist. In 2010, she retired as an administrator and executive director of the Native Hawaiian Legal Corporation after 32 years. The corporation is a six-attorney public interest law firm specialising in indigenous rights. She has published in many literary journals and anthologies. In 1993, she received the Elliot Cades Award for literature. Her first book of poetry, *Uluhaimalama*, was published in 2008. She and her husband, Ed, a native farmer, reside on the island of Maui. They have seven children and fourteen grandchildren.

Ed's Hoʻokupu

A gift for Mōʻī Wahine,
Wahine Kapu,
An offering, hoʻokupu,
From Wailuanui
Of the thundering seacliffs;
Wailuanui
Of the upright canoes;
A gift for Beloved Liliʻulani.
This morning
Maui raised its sun
Over Haleakalā,
The Koʻolau mountains.
The Ῑʻaleʻale winds scattered;
The great rains,
The clattering ʻiliʻili
Were silenced.
At Moku Mana
White ribboned ʻIwa
Soared, borne aloft,
While the teeming moi
Shone silver, silver,
Shimmering glass
Beside Long Stone
At the muliwai.
This morning

Ed went up mauka
To Lakini
Where as a boy
After bright days
Tending lo'i
He would catch a glimpse
Through forbidden window
Of red and yellow opulence,
The sacred 'ahu'ula, kapu,
Its feathered brilliance
Hung across
The dark parlor wall
Of Tūtū Samson's old hale.
Even then,
St Gabriel's Church
Loomed stark
Amidst this surround
Of holy waters.
Now Tūtū Elena's lokelani
Imparts a rosy sweetness
To the Wailua 'ulu
Known for its fragrance.
This morning with Carl,
Ed picked the great Queens,
Crimson ginger torches
Brightly lit
Along the meandering 'auwai;
And from the lo'i kalo,
Tended by Lance,
He gathered tender 'oha,
Huli intact,
Each green heart as open
As a dutiful son's.
Last night,
The kani of great rains;
Ed took a flask
Of anointing waters
From above the place where
Waiokamilo flows past roseapple.
From the picture window
At Wailua homestead
A thundering waterfall,
The great heart of Waiokāne
Still beating.

Kalua

I

Sometimes I imagine
The grey corpses
Of early missionaries
Stirring lustily
In their vaults
Joining in
A rousing rendition
Of 'Kalua'
The song from
Birds of Paradise
That Hollywood yarn
Starring bromide white
Deborah Paget
Who conjured up
A native woman
About to be sacrificed
To the great volcano god
By heathen Hawaiians
Somehow it seems fitting
Since missionaries
Brought that pilau
That they should fugue off –
Organist
Choir
Congregation
Included
(This is the night of love
This is the hour of
Kaa-luuuuuu-ah –)

II

Whenever ma and Auntie Liz
Sang that song
Tūtū would scold
'A'ole maika'i kēlā hīmeni!
Meaning
That song is no good
Or more to the point
That song
Is not Hawaiian

She and the girls
Would kui lei
On the front porch
Of the old house
On Cummins Street
For boat days
Then they would sing
       Ku'u Pua i Paoakalani,
       Kamalani o Keaukaha,
       Kalama'ula –
But the sweet fragrance
Of those long ago gardens
Would soon disappear
Following Deborah Paget
To cinder and ash
Mother
What did you know
How could you know
Sneaking movies
At Kewalo theatre
Except to lose
Hawaiian skin, lips, hair, heft –
Hollywood,
after all
Wasn't about to save you
From volcano sacrifice.

III
In the 1940s and '50s
All along Honolulu Harbor
The old Hawaiian stevedores
Would kanikapila
Late into the night
They would gather
       At Mokauea
       At Kewalo
       At Kālia
Lifting sweet harmonies
To ocean, wind, stars
This was before
Walter Dillingham dredged
Caul and skull
Crushed and cured

For pavement
This was before
His asphyxiate tar
Blackened everything
This was before
Union bosses
Buried dissidents
In hotel footings
Then called in the kahu
To bless them
This was when Waikīkī
Was ringed with loko iʻa
And throw nets filled with
ʻĀholehole, ʻanae, ʻaʻama
Were commonplace
Those days
Must have been sweet.

Liliʻu

We are singing a requiem for our mother,
Our voices a shroud across this land
Wrenched we were, from Kamakaʻehaʻs soft bosom,
Wretched, our grief inconsolable
We are feeble scratchings against cold granite vaults,
Grasping, tremulous as moondark trees,
Our fire-spirits burned black as cinders –
Our mouths filled with ash.

Our motherʻs spirit was incandescent colour, Green
Ocean of emerald stars, mosses, living grass:
Know you our sweet-voiced mother?
Know you her childrenʻs sorrow?
Cloudless azure, blue-veined petal:
Her blood was a firebrand night,
Her bones iridescent light;
She sang the sunlit bird.

Fire-spirits burned black as cinders,
Mouths filled with ash,
We search the empty garden, Uluhaimalama,
Papery flowers on melancholy earth. Now

Our song is for our mother,
Our nation,
Our rebirth.

LEIALOHA PERKINS

Leialoha Apo Perkins is a retired professor of Hawaiian studies from the
University of Hawai'i who holds a PhD from the University of Pennsylvania.
A poet, short-story writer, novelist, editor and scholarly critic, she is the author of
Kingdoms of the Heart, Histories in Stone, Wood, Bone (poetry), *Natural, Firemakers
and Other Short Stories of Hawai'i, the Sāmoas, and Tonga* (short stories), *The Oxridge
Woman* (novel) and editor of the two volumes of the *Journal of Hawaiian and Pacific
Folklore and Folklife Studies*.

How the 'Iva Flies

I will not hold my breath
as the ocean rolls its long
and silver tongue sweeping to death
the land in lilting song.

I will not shut my eyes
to the rags of spindrift
the shark's clean cruising streak
and how the 'Iva flies

crying
from cliff to littoral.

Waving seaweeds desolate
in dance I know and I know not
because there is a singing in everything
and green is the colour of the heart.

RUPERAKE PETAIA

Poet Ruperake Petaia was educated mainly in Sāmoa, except for a four-year eternity studying at the University of the South Pacific, Fiji, after which he was awarded a piece of paper to decorate his parents' home. He worked as a public servant for almost thirty years and then studied theology for four years. Following this, he was editor of the newsletter of the Congregational Christian Church in Sāmoa, *O le Sulu Samoa*, for one and a half years, then manager of the Church's printing press for two years. He is presently the pastor of a church parish in Sāmoa.

A Pain with a Butt

Observe, these callous clouds;
fusty flakes off the bitter blues
of morbid-eyed monsters
puffing foul air over
an otherwise
decent morning chat;

Consider, those nicotine-laden
brown jaws putrid to the vein clots
of bloody mutant mugs spraying
vile vapour from an otherwise
plain old afternoon yawn,

and watch, those bloated nostrils
rumbling in melted mucus
stale as cowshit in a drizzle
spewing from an otherwise
sweet smile of a perfect
evening:

those niggles aside,
I swear I could well
have saved your day,
pardoning the fact
you were once
a pain with a butt.

Primitive Thinking Things, Animals

Primitive thinking things, animals
they hunt in packs
and they travel in flocks;
they swim in shoals
and they build in hordes;

they dwell in the darkest jungles
and in the deepest oceans and valleys;
they roam from season to season
and they live off their God-given
spares by the day:

Yet, they never build armies
to destroy themselves
like primitive thinking people do.

Our Past

Much of our past
is like a good thriller,
best remembered
for the countless
nightmares we keep
burying in the graves
of our sleepless nights:

the few moments
of relief will at least
see the hero scrambling
out of the terror into
a likely future sequel.

A Stuck-Up

According to popular definition
a stuck-up is a facelift
glued to the sky
looking down
on the world.

From a vertical distance,
the only things visible
are the nostrils
turning up
to hold the nose
from running down:

the rest of its body
hiding in the clouds,
squirms like a frightened
chicken scared of heights.

A passer-by observing
that sully mug,
was insincerely hoping
the glue might hold.

KIRI PIAHANA-WONG

Kiri Piahana-Wong is a New Zealander of Māori (Ngāti Ranginui), English and Chinese ancestry. She is an editor, poet, writer, ESOL teacher and lawyer; and runs Anahera Press, the mission of which is to publish writing in all genres that promotes cross-cultural understanding. Kiri is also a performance poet, and MC at Poetry Live, New Zealand's longest-running live poetry venue. In her spare time, she can be found checking out the surf at Piha Beach.

It was a time of heartbreak
Ka pā mai te pouri i taua wā

It was a hard year.
My sister's mental illness. My
mother's poor health. New lines
on my father's face.

I lost my ability to
write, and, for a while, to
talk. I inhabited my own head. I
felt very alone.

I interspersed reading the
Bible with reading Jenny
Bornholdt's *These Days*.
I think Jenny helped me
more, although I liked
Psalm 69. In this psalm,
David is going through a
terrible time, and it made me
feel marginally better, like
watching news about
famine in Africa, and realising
we have a cupboard full
of food, plenty of water,
and a house that doesn't
leak (except in particularly
heavy rain).

I concentrated hard on the small
things: like keeping myself
warm. I wrapped
myself in poetry and
merino fingerless gloves.
Whenever the sun came out,
I ran outside and basked,
alongside my cat. We
would do this 4–5 times
a day, until the sun
went away.

It helped.
A little.

Hoki atu ki ō maunga kia purea ai e ngā hau a Tāwhirimātea.
Return to the mountain. Let the winds of Tāwhirimātea refresh you.

Deep Water Talk
in honour of Hone Tuwhare
for Melinda, Sophie & Nathan

& no one knows
if your eyes are
blurred red from
the wind, too
much sun, or the
tears streaking your
face that could be
tears or just lines of
dried salt, who
can tell

& you never can tell
if you are seasick,
drunk, or just
hungover – the
symptoms are the
same

& sea and sky merge
until the horizon is

nothing but an
endless blue line
in every direction,
so that you are sailing,
not on the sea, as you
thought, but in a
perfectly blue, circular
bowl, never leaving
the centre

& you wonder who is
moving, you or
the clouds racing
by the mast-head

& you wonder if
those dark shapes
in the water are
sharks, shadows, or
nothing but old fears
chasing along behind
you

& the great mass of
land recedes, until
you forget you were
a land-dweller, and
you start feeling the
pull of ancient genes
– in every tide, your
blood sings against
the moon

& food never tasted
so good, or water
so sweet – you've
never conserved water
by drinking wine
before – and rum;
and coke; and rum
and coke; and can
after can of cold
beer

& your sleep is
accompanied, not
by the roar of traffic
on the highway,
but by the creaks
and twangs of your
ship as she pitches
and moans through
the dark ocean,
all alone

& you wonder –
where did that bird,
that great gull perching
on the bowsprit,
come from?

TIARE PICARD

Tiare Picard was born in Honolulu, Hawai'i and received her MA from the University of Hawai'i at Mānoa. Her poetry has appeared in Tinfish Press's *Tinfish 18.5: Poetry, Puzzles and Games* (2008), *Ka Lamakua, Ka Leo O Hawai`i, The Honolulu Weekly, Achiote Press* and *Hawai`i Review*, and poems are forthcoming in *Tinfish 20* (2010). Tiare is a co-founder of Fat Ulu, a literary hui dedicated to the arts and literature in Hawai'i. In 2009, she edited their debut publication, *The Statehood Project: Spontaneous Collaboration*. Tiare lives her with mother in 'Aiea, and adores her cat Cujo.

Ancestors

Hooks catch more than fish:
swiftness of air, salt in a wave,
lucid dreams of old women.
One stands on a southern atoll,
a second straddles the Southeast.
One more knows snow.

Tricksters in shadows, they find
comfort in the trenched curves
of fingerprints on jade,
among folds of muscle, the *O* in a stone.

They speak in monotones
wrapped in envelopes of Hanafuda
colours, or chimed in key chains
made of balsam; in trickled nut milk
through cheesecloth
or purple yarn at the loom,

smooth and soft like a head of hair.

The Tower

A bird clicks her foreign tongue • her
sliver-tongue clicks • I am lost
in her redundant locution.

I cannot click my flat tongue • I am deaf
to the pink • of her tongue • I click
my pen instead • and invent a word
for her tongue's klick.

Meanwhile, beetles feast on my ink • they
klick a different klick (they have no tongues
to klick) • they cradle my klick to swollen
abdomens • scurry across the linoleum •
and klick-up new and improved cliques.

We three flounder this way • for clicks upon
klicks, upon cliques • each spewing louder
than the former • each mis • construing
the other.

Clicking our way to Etemenanki, the bird
falls silent first • upset, you see • for
she meant *cli* • she thrusts her beak
into abdomens • silencing the *qu*
of the beetles' clique.

She swings low and sings her *cli* •
then swallows my flat tongue licking
her sliver-tongue's click.

Friday

except that fences now stretch
across the meridian, gateposts smell of urine

meander, cross Roosevelt Memorial
Bridge, or Ford Island Bridge, coral roads
that arc for Pape'ete or Majuro, negotiate
at break neck speed through the 1948
Armistice Agreement Line.

In the back seat
where maps are conceived,
knuckles graze cuffed sleeves, and hands
open for marked persimmons, a pear,
or breadfruit balled-up and sour.

Given the number of prefixes
available for plucking,
an ism is an ending
but not the end.

Platoon

Shell Vacation's Waikīkī Resort Sends Packages to US Troops in Iraq.
One vacation ownership resort on Waikīkī has found
an ideal and patriotic use for its small bottled toiletry items
by sending them to US troops in Iraq.

One vacation ownership resort on Waikīkī has found
5 cheap thrills on Kaua'i
by sending them to US troops in Iraq.
Kāne'ohe Marines await their turn at war.

5 cheap thrills on Kaua'i.
Any sane individual would prefer the white

sandy beaches of Waikīkī over northern Iraq.
Kāneʻohe Marines await their turn at war.
The Marine Corps, stretched thin by two wars.

Any sane individual would prefer the white
                sandy beaches of Waikīkī over northern Iraq.
At least two Hawaiʻi Marines are killed.
The Marine Corps, stretched thin by two wars
                on a MySpace web page.

At least two Hawaiʻi Marines are killed
keeping ʻem rolling, managing Pōhakuloa, rebuilding Iraq.
On a MySpace web page,
Warner says he lives on the Marine Corps Base Hawaiʻi.

Keeping ʻem rolling, managing Pōhakuloa, rebuilding Iraq.
The site of an army training area in the saddle between
                Mauna Loa and Mauna Kea.
Warner says he lives on the Marine Corps Base, Hawaiʻi.
7000 Marines of Marine Corps Base Hawaiʻi remain ready
                at Kāneʻohe Bay.

The site of an army training area in the saddle between
                Mauna Loa and Mauna Loa.
Shell Vacation's Waikīkī Resort Sends Packages to US Troops in Iraq.
7000 Marines of Marine Corps Base, Hawaiʻi remain ready
                at Kāneʻohe Bay –

ideal and patriotic use for its small bottled toiletry items.

TAFEA POLAMALU

In addition to European and Native American ancestry, Tafea Polamalu has ancestral ties to the island of Ta'ū in Manua. He was raised in the blue-collar rural town of Tenmile in the mountains of Southwest Oregon. He worked for thirteen years as a wild-land firefighter. He is currently living in Oregon raising his two beautiful daughters: Milaneta and Maleata.

Afakasi Philosophy

I used to carry my Sāmoaness like
a mouth-full of salty semen: never knowing
whether to spit or swallow.

But that is the ethos of a *halfy*, right?
Born on a twilight shoreline, unable to define
land from sea or darkness from light

Because *half* is less than *whole*, right?
At least, this is how we are made to feel.
So unfold your collar to hide your gills and
wear closed-toed shoes so society will not see
your freakish webbed feet

Or,

I have a better idea,
let's blow cum bubbles at
other peoples' troubles and
celebrate our amphibious identities

Daddy Said

Son,
I prunk you hea
pecause tis is ta lan of
opprotunity

In Samoa,
te is nofing
To you heard me Son?
nofing

Hea in Ameika,
ta worlt is at
you finka tip
and ta sky is ta limits

You know why I nefa
teach you Samoan Son?
cause Samoan no ket you
anyfing in life

tis is ta white man's worlt
an Enklish is
only fink tat matta

You heard me Son?

Tis is ta white man's worlt
an at ta en of ta tay, we all haf
to walk fru his toor

at ta en of ta tay, we all haf
walk fru his toor
cause he sign ta check Son

look at me,
my whole life i strukle wif
fo try speak ta Enklish

i strukle my ass off Son
so tat you can ket you
pestes echucation

So i make tamn sure
my sons masta Enklish
pecause tis is what pestes

You see what I'm said Son?

Tis is why it pisses me when
te say, 'How come I nefa teachet
you speak Samoan?'

What ta hell te fink I prunk you here fo eh?
tes stupit hets know
nofing apout Samoa

Rememper sumfing Son,
Ameika is ta pestes place in ta worlt
so ket ta echucation

pe ta tocto
pe ta lawya
tis is my tream fo you
tis is why fo i prunk you hea

fo to kif you ta
opprotunity to haf ta
fings i nefa haf

You see what I'm said Son?

Okay, koot talk
alu su'esu'e
ko prush ta teef
an to ta maf homewok

Nifo Oti

1

You no longer drip
the sweet war blood of
your enemies

You no longer hang their
freshly severed heads
from your lave:
hook-shaped fang

Nifo oti

Tonight
the aitus call your name!

2

Tooth of Death
in a colonial breath
you have 'progressed' from
wood-bone flesh
to stainless steel

You have moved
from the art of killing to
the art of dancing and
traded red blood for
blue flame

No one knows your name or
remembers your former life
they now call you the 'fire knife'

3

Siva Afi
Fire Dance

'Ailao
Knife Dance

'Ailao Afi
Fire Knife Dance

Warrior from then: that pre-Christ dark age
time warped to now: today
you dance on your stage cage
for minimum wage
what is the source of
your rage?

They say,
just smile and spin your
savage knife

you are here to woo
papālagi eyes

You know the routine,
spin, break, under the legs
around the head
side to side, between the legs
toss and catch behind the back . . .

Hear the oooos and aaaaahs
hear the pate and the lali drumming
don't forget to smile because
a pleasant-faced savage keeps
the tourists cumming

Thank You Colonialism For:

Jesus and Crack
Duct Tape and SPAM
Elongated Lifespans and Artificial Tans
Tongue Scrapers and Anthrax
401Ks and Bikini Wax
Bougainville and Big Macs
Pi = 3.14159 and Colostomy Bags
Abu Ghraib and Breast Implants
Joe Camel and Uncle Sam
Hiroshima and Styrofoam
Anthropology and the Tijuana Donkey Show
Dangling Modifiers and the World Bank
The Equator and Swank
Vasectomies and Segways
Six-Legged Frogs and the KKK
Mad Cow and Columbus Day
Facebook and the Southeast Asian Sex Trade
'Counter Terrorism' and 'Failed States'
Jersey Shore and Blue Ray
The Greenhouse Effect and Preparation H
The MEF and the GRA
The US–Mexican Border and Menthols
Sputnik and Cubicles
Bernie Madoff and Urinals
Rogaine and Wall Street

The Easter Bunny and Wounded Knee
Dick Cheney and Anal Beads
The Jewish State of Israel and Anabolic Steroids
The Invention of the 'Savage' and Suppositories
Dog the Bounty Hunter and YouTube
Skin-Whitening Bleach and Sinking Tuvalu
Throw Pillows and Spermacide
Halliburton and *Pimp My Ride*
Archdiocese Paedophilia and Uranium-235
Fox News and Sound Bites
The Panama Canal and Astroglide
The Indian Removal Act and Twitter
The 'Discovery' of the Pacific Ocean and Lucifer
Liposuction and Disposable Diapers
Survivor Samoa and Pacemakers
The Middle Passage and the My Lai Massacre
The Electric Chair and Henry Kissinger
Jim Crow Laws and the Polynesian Cultural Center
The Invention of the 'Nigger' and the Federal Reserve
'Don't Ask, Don't Tell' and Darfur
Manifest Destiny and the Hunt for Assata Shakur
Smallpox Blankets and the Twisted Double Helix
Reaganomics and Sherm Sticks
The Ho Chi Minh Trail and the Jena Six
Laser Eye Surgery and G-Strings
Super Big Gulps and the Letter 'Z'
iPods and H3s
The CIA and MP3s
SUVs and PCP
PNG and AIG
The FBI and ATVs
ATMs and PS3s
FOBs and M16s
The LAPD and RPGs
WOW and MSG
The ATF and LCD HD TVs
PTSD and WMDs
East Timor and Waikīkī
The NRA and Skeet Skeet Skeet
OPEC and the WTO
The Invention of the 'Third World' and CEOs
Battery-Operated Nasal Clippers and HMO
Eight-Minute Abs and *The Electric Kool-Aid Acid Test*
The Teabaggers and Identity Theft

Blackwater and Glenn Beck
Viagra and the Age of Enlightenment
1-800-GET-U-SUM and Kevlar Vests
Red Bull and the Tuskegee Experiment
Artificial Insemination and *Rambo*
Sexting and Waco
Enemas and Castle Bravo
Blood Diamonds and the Alamo
Katrina and XM Radio
The Name 'New Zealand' and Drano
Lobotomies and Mobile Homes
Tribal Identification Cards and Guantánamo
Syphilis and George W. Bush
The Mormon Tabernacle Choir and Hydroponic Purple Kush
Ass-less Chaps and Captain Cook
Lygers and Corn Dogs
Drone Attacks and Enron
The Great Melting Pot and Botox
CNMI and Flight 77
Free Trade and 9/11
Hell and Heaven
The Immaculate Conception and the International Space Station
Erectile Disfunction Medication and One Nation
Under God
Indivisible
With Liberty
And Justice for All

DOUG POOLE

Doug Poole is of Sāmoan (Ulberg āiga of Tula'ele, Apia, Upolu) and European descent. He resides in Waitakere City, Auckland, with his wife, Anja, and their three children. He is the current e-publisher and editor of poetry e-zine Blackmail Press (www.blackmailpress.com/index.html). Doug has been e-published in *Trout*, *OBAN 06* and *Fugacity* at the nzepc, *Soft Blow*, *Nexus Collection* and many other electronic publications, as well as *Niu Voices* (Huia) and *Landfall 218*, edited by David Eggleton. Doug produced the Creative New Zealand Pacific Arts Board-funded performance poetry show *POLYNATION*, performed at the Queensland Poetry Festival 2008 and Going West Books and Writers Festival 2008. You can contact Doug by email: editor@blackmailpress.com.

Posala & Gogo'sina III

There is a gecko in our room
it watches us every night so
I cover my underpants
with an 'ie lavalava, 'cause
you never know it could be
a relative or someone
we don't know
Gogo'sina says, it is
good luck to have her
I think to myself it looks
like a boy, 'cause he just
stays there all night
hiding from the flying
fox who hangs upside
down outside our window

On the underside of a breadfruit
leaf is a white tree snail
listening to the flying fox
dream; memorising the
genealogy escaping
as sleep talk, but
Gogo'sina says

it is just the breeze
coming in through
the window
The chickens sleep too
I wonder if they know
we are leaving next week?
Gogo'sina says go to sleep
We're shopping in Apia tomorrow

Pouliuli 4

He smacked her in
the mouth, strangled her
on the lounge room floor,
she, the great granddaughter
of a high chief of Safune.

Down the front steps
crushed-cash tumbleweeds
are we coconut offspring
of an English gentleman?

Just take the bloody money.

He rolls down the front stairs
crashes next door to borrow
a cigarette, bruises his arms
back, legs, an' Peter just laughs;
smiles the smile darkness fears.

He falls into the colonial light
of red lions & factory floors
lucky dips, benefit draws,
bets on the horses on 'Amelikan' cars
wakes in pouliuli banging.

Open the fucking door!

There is terror in her
eyes as the front door pane
gives way to a stupor fist.
Up late, her son sits

on the river of blood
poured over his head.
The sink turns blood-
red and shakes.

Gogolo

to Karlo Mila

You, are the black butterfly
gracing our sleeping mouths
your words retrace movements
beneath the feet of ancestors
folds, to sit within cinematic Va

You, are the blue taupou,
her courage to shake the
frigates from her back
fingertips shattered pearls;
words the gogolo of tidal rain

are you listening to the singing scales of Va
before Tagaloaalagi split the stone
unimpeded by gravity, the thin ear

You, break the shackles of oppression,
giving Rangatahi expression
partaking in your heart; words
from your open hands soaring

BRIAN POTIKI

Born in New Zealand in 1953 into the Kāi Tahu, Kāti Māmoe tribe, Brian lives near Rotorua. He has written, directed and acted in five history plays (*South of the Titi Islands, Motupohue, A Mutiny Stripped, Boultbee, Hiroki's Song*) set in the South Island and in 2009 finished *Maranga Mai: Radical Maori Theatre in the 1980s*, a book about the play *Maranga Mai*, a seminal work of Māori theatre from 1980 to 1981 that he directed, co-wrote and acted in. His book of poems and songs, *Aotearoa*, was published in 2003 and a book of plays, *Te Waipounamu, Your Music Remembers Me*, in 2007.

for tim buckley

sometimes the softest whisper
would deafen the storms that were coming
our lovemaking swelled the silence
rippling like an angry wind
the ripples felt like waves

on the surface of our dreams
there was sweat
& on the leaves
of the flowers
you could hear sweet music
when the flowers were opened
by the melancholy moon
& the graveyard sun

i've been thinking about you tonight
& the women who loved me until their love died
since you left the party hasn't stopped
& it's taken just about all we've got

tribal

i

we gave them kai &
carried pots of pūhā & meat
up the steps of the fleahouse

we stood our tents across from ngāti pōneke marae
& were arrested

we waited in court
with our sisters from the sunset
who steer the jap sailors up to their rooms
with honey-tongued japanese –
shit it was so pathetic

wake up wake up
to the blue tatts on our kids
their hands arms & faces
look like a rotten kai
the rats have eaten

stick your ear into their party
get smashed stoned drunk to the bottomless funk
they sway to asleep & waking, zunk !
& wake up wake up

when the shit's falling thick
take a piece of wood &
shove it up the tiko hole of justice –
put a sharp point on it
like an old throwing spear

aroha your brothers & sisters
for their good heart
& hate the laws that
cut them down &
squash them into pulp –
wake up wake up

ii

thirty standing round a blue & white zephyr
thirty men in jackets that read Black Power

thirty minds bent like an iron bar
thirty with burning black sight
thirty with a stone in the guts
thirty smashed hearts
thirty gangs knit the broken-minded boys

with knives of fear
steel fists of mana
heavy boots of bone
black parents of heavy chain

shaven headed boys sitting in the railway station
shaven headed boys going to ōtaki
shaven headed boys going to see their girlfriend
shaven headed boys herded to the pub
shaven headed boys made to get drunk
shaven headed boys herded into a stolen car
shaven headed boys driving under a truck
shaven headed boys going to the funeral

suddenly the doors were blocked
suddenly a small group covered the doors
suddenly the sāmoans moved &
suddenly they were holding michael taingahue
suddenly mark godinet swung &
suddenly the sixteen year old stopped protesting
suddenly the boy's mouth stopped roaring
suddenly the boy's head went *slap!*
suddenly they lifted him off the steps
suddenly they buried him in taranaki

shaven headed boys herded out to stand in the rain
shaven headed boys initiated into the gang
shaven headed boys eat the gang sandwich
(a man lowers his jeans &
drops his shit between two pieces of bread
for the new boy &
he eats the sandwich)

hiroki's song

i know i have four more days to live
as i dreamt the other night
i am to be hanged
tēnā koe te whiti

they will not try you these pākehā
they break their promises
think of me
tēnā koe te whiti

a pākehā came to defend me
on the day before the trial
there were no friends
tēnā koe te whiti

i asked the court when i could speak
they said after the lawyer has finished
i was not asked
tēnā koe te whiti

i waited for them to ask me
the judge put on his black cap
to pass sentence on me
tēnā koe te whiti

hearts

bob, what haven't i told you?
that tony fomison once described you as *that ego-less poet*
& the Sāmoan at wellington or auckland railway station
called you that guy who's always reading a book . . .
i already told you that!
i'm feeling good after your visit is all
you walked to meet us . . . i was a bit jumpy –
i'd just yelled at my son on the lake
(in front of his friend)
then i saw the guinness you'd brought
shining on the table like a gang of fleas
we hugged

i have your benediction next to me in the caravan –
don't be so disgruntled
you should know by now
that cold mountain
is anywhere & everywhere
– alongside verlaine to rimbaud (1872)
& *volcano* by derek walcott
i love you e hoa

soon – two weeks – i'm going to māori heaven (te kaha):
i'll go like a man . . . an ape!
like a hairy fuck-up carrying all the gifts (cohen, mingus,
sullivan, lorca, murakami etc.) you ever sent me
& my guitar

hey bob, i'll be singing in the beer tent
breathing all over selwyn . . .
getting him to play *you don't know me*
which i'll sing like a whale or a tibetan monk
while hone gives the thumbs up from the corner
& para passes round the rum (which
we drink from the cap *à la* pule)

you wanna come?

ROMA PŌTIKI

Born in Lower Hutt, New Zealand in 1958, Roma Pōtiki's tribal affiliations are to Te Rarawa, Te Aupōuri and Ngāti Rangitihi. She is a playwright and commentator on Māori theatre, and has been a theatre performer and director of a Māori theatre company. Roma is also a curator and visual artist and has work in the permanent collection of TheNewDowse in Lower Hutt. Her published poetry includes the collections *Stones in Her Mouth* (IWA for New Women's Press, 1992), *Shaking the Tree* (Steele Roberts, 1998) and *Oriori* (Tandem Press, 1999), a collaboration with visual artist Robyn Kahukiwa. Her work has been widely anthologised.

Cannibals

Stopping in the dark
on a back-country road
and being led by uncle
to his favourite mystery.

At first you're not sure
why you're here and what you're meant to see,
but he is so eager.

Your hands reach out tentatively
into the soft black and you slide your feet slowly,
edge along the thin trail, careful, careful not to slip.

I can't see anything
look up to the sky – no promises there,
nothing on either side either.

Then, as my eyes keep searching, I notice them,
the big show-offs.

All along the damp-earthed bank
blue incandescent lights strung about the ferns
a luminous and elusive veil.

'They have a sticky thread, just one hanging off them,' he says. 'That's how they catch their prey. And if one of their own touches the thread they'll eat them too. That's right – we're surrounded by a pack of bloody cannibals! Cannibals! What d'ya think of that then?'

I don't speak. It's very quiet when uncle stops talking.

Quiet, and full with the night smells,
the shadows, the soft, beautiful cannibals.

Down we go

Here at the end of sleep, you arrive again, not suddenly but slipping beside me as though you are some other life I have not yet understood. A smile moves across my face. Kēhua rock the branches above our silence and there is intimacy, like standing barefoot on a slatted wooden mat, like being enveloped by rising steam.

She comes to visit me now
the lingering essence of violets
a worn cream dress printed with English flowers.

I see her, the wisps of soft hair
caught loosely with pins and net,
high colour in the cheeks
and a smile that seems so far away
as though it were floating on a festooned ship
back home to the old city.

She is walking amongst the rockery
picking her way through bluebells, sweet william, and peppery carnations.
Small lizards scatter at her approach, find another place to wait.
I follow behind, harnessed in invisible traces –
down we go, under the old lemon, past the wild japonica hedge
and here, sitting together, eating cake beneath the kōwhai.

Later, after sugary tea and sun have done their job
I fold, head down on her apron pocket.

In the evening kitchen it is nearly dark.
We eat bread with greengage jam.
I brush the hot sun and garden smell from her hair.

After a bath we pomade ourselves with Yardley.
We don't speak much,
I just watch her
and she seems pleased with me.

I fall asleep
as the ageing Singer
pieces a swathe of patterns
into dreams . . .
a bonnet for Pearl's baby, a skirt for Mary,
a shirred summer dress for Grace
and Corinne, well it won't make any difference what that madam wears,
it'll all turn out the same.

*There is no moon. I sit hunched in the kōwhai tree, clutching a white purse. The clasp breaks and out
fall buttons, bright threads and nutmeg, metal buckles in the shape of birds, a tinkling sherry glass,
letters that the ink has never dried on. You are standing at the edge of the deepest river, waving.*

Speaking out

To all the smug men
who think that speaking the reo is going to save them
who think that language makes them one better than someone else
particularly women.

To all the men who think that just being born
and speaking our own language
is enough
I'm telling you it's not.

No, it's not enough,
though it may win you a job in the new corporation
it may mean that Pākehā ask your advice and pay you
it may mean that Māori women who are intimidated by your supposed
knowledge
bow and curtail
and perhaps even sleep with you and have your children.

Getting a tohu degree means something,
but it doesn't give you the right to make others feel less-than-you
less than you in your new-found opulence
pounamu-coloured opulence, Apple Mac opulence
citing your 'boil-up' past or your oppression.

You don't impress me
though I admire hard work and persistence, intelligence and
the ability to get things done.
it doesn't impress me if it tells lies about women,
if it ignores children, if it is so rigid
that it forgets justice in the insecure worry
that we will 'lose everything'.

In the rush to retain tradition I've even heard some men
(and women)
say that
women don't do the haka. What nonsense.
We always did, we always will.

For the truth to be told about a culture all parties have to be
in on it.
Especially if you want it to survive in a useful form.
So,
don't use the language as a weapon against each other.
It's a taonga, one of many,
not a gold Rolex fixed in one position.
Who defines time anyway?

JOHN PULE

John Pule was born in 1962 on the family land of Pia in the village of Liku on Niue. He arrived in Aotearoa New Zealand in 1964 and held a number of labouring jobs before he started writing poetry in 1980. He has published poetry and prose, and his publications include *Winter, the Rain* (1981), *The Shark That Ate the Sun* (1992), *Burn my Head in Heaven* (1998) and *Bond of Time* (1998), as well as a collaboration with Nicholas Thomas, *Hiapo: Past and Present in Niuean Barkcloth* (2005). He received the Pacific Island Arts Award in 1996. John Pule has been writer in residence at the University of Waikato (1996), the University of the South Pacific (1997), the University of Auckland (2000), the University of Hawai'i at Mānoa (2002); and artist in residence at the Oceania Centre for Arts & Culture, USP (1997–2006), the Cultural Museum, Rarotonga (2004) and the University of Canterbury (1998). In 2004 he was honoured with a Laureate Award by the Arts Foundation of New Zealand. *Hauaga*, a book on his art, was released by Otago University Press in June 2010, to coincide with the first major survey exhibition of John Pule's work, curated by the City Gallery, Wellington.

Midnight Oceans

Karekare, 05/01/05

What is a rock like me
doing in a small forest?
being on the coast I should be
where the sea brings news.

My mind sways the way I like
between oblivion and joy
the wind for example
tells me I am mythical.

Then again the music I hear
is a reminder of the years I
have spent pondering death.

That cloud is my friend I don't know
that sun-ray is my god I think
whether that falling leaf is my end.

Inter-islander (in Kaikōura), 06/05

it was the sea I dived into
sharks sensed my urgency
my hands the clouds succumbed to
the lives of stones pulsating.
my head I tried to rise
and understand these memories
climbing mountains
towards god,
carrying one wing, heart

I want to live for you
there will be another time to parachute
not today
nor tomorrow

Suva, 17/06/06

South Sea morning 3 a.m.
what am I, who close your eyes
I am, and I am alive
if I am he, let my soul agree
purpose is a hopeful time
a kind of leaf, a big hiss
a mountain I painted by yawning
yes, I know I am a glow,
bleeding as I grow,
not from the black star
running. I go.

Suva, Saturday, 2006

You told me once, you cannot satisfy me,
there was a time when I was a stone
my soil was made of memory
at times a brilliant sun shone on me

instead of dying, I said, I want to live,
I stood up, threw a bottle into
the dark, afterwards, when I was
drunk I masturbated, yes,

I spilled a sperm capable of
a baby, forcing its liver to induce
a country made of paper and air,

when I was lost, tempted my lungs,
to explode. Every day I ran
into a beautiful Pacific Ocean.

Suva, 2006
to my daughter

On the early hours of Thursday morning
around 1 a.m., I grabbed an
18-year-bottle of Glenfiddich
and proceeded to drink.
That morning was the 24th of August,
your birthday, you would be 14 years
old today.
I danced and sang, not realising
it was the day you were born
in that late afternoon – in Grey Lynn, in 1992.

I fell asleep at 4.30 a.m.

Your mother called me at work at 9 a.m.,
she cried. I did too, the ocean
between us, you, her, me.

A candle was lit for you in Auckland
and in my office in Suva.

I will join you eventually
that makes me content
knowing you, again

Auckland, 18/04/08

When a small light finds
me, it is the sun
or a magnificent tree
reminds me that my hands
could still hold that first flower
which grew at my mouth
which drew
breath from a nameless petal

that sun was a reflection
that showed itself in glass
I slept, woke up, slept,
woke up and slept till dawn
I am an ocean
that had a broken heart
that let the first saliva
make itself known as an airplane

Auckland, 24/08/08

To the sea we drove
in a day of rain and clouds
and in that small time
yes we cried

the sea called us
we threw red carnations
the waves ate the lollies
yes we cried

returning to the city
it was possible
to go to heaven
and even there we will keep on crying

Auckland, 29/12/08

You cannot hold the wind down,
is how my sister described my life.
You have always been a free spirit.
A fire lit up, then quickly died.

The raw smoke emanating from it
joined the clouds above,
careful not to knock my tongue
as a puff left my mouth.

Yes, that's the story of a stone,
in my mother's pocket I arrived
carried from house to house,

hospitals, doctors, police stations,
courts, detention centres, jails, funerals,
a legacy of an invisible dream.

another day as a stone
as a piece of nothing amongst
crowded insects
sun beam is a broken axle
but I must ride it

a centre of a poet's life
is just another form of fruit
the core if anyone dares to look
is a dark hill where grows
a stubby tree

one bird lives there
as a messenger of a lucky sky,
should, if I do not give in,
sing the most glorious song
to free me from this earth

TAGI QOLOUVAKI

Tagi is Fijian/Tongan on her mum's side and German/English American on her dad's – altogether a very mixed, queer and feminist PI. Born and raised in Fiji by a few beautiful men and many powerful women, she migrated to the United States aged sixteen. Now, twenty years later, she plans to move back to the islands, to study and teach and pen a few more poems.

Untitled

how do i describe
how my body wakes, moves
to the heat of your words . . .
like pele's footprints waken kīlauea.

your words so hot they're molten
syllables slip and slide, thickly,
stir my depths
shift plates between our nations
send your seas against my shores.
your tongue, your vowels,
so deep i ride waves against and through them
my skin become your ocean
your blood my tide . . .

i tattoo you with teeth and nails
dreams and tongue;
tattoo you deeply
stories old and new
into the skin of my heart
in indigo, in ink,
with shell lip and coral dust
memory and desire . . .
i will trace lines
undulating
spiralling
reaching
like our bodies for each other . . .
yes, deeply
into skin
lips, tongue and breath, till
my scent becomes yours
your texture mine

your words
quicken
my blood-tissue-cells

like pele
i am ready
to birth new islands
darken fresh soil
with this love . . .

we will grow frangipani
with creamy yellow centres
papaya and blue taro
sugarcane and mangoes
. . . with this love

Tell Me a Story

He vows I am planted beneath the Frangipani
Promises I am seeded beneath the Bua.

He has his father's tongue,
Owns his mother's languages.
They sing honeyed songs together.
He has even tamed the pālagi one –
It rides his tongue
And he is fertile with story.

Deftly, he weaves tales
Like the finest mats
Constructs memories
Tapa-tapestries
Stained in soil and
Colored with song.

We store them,
Cultural currency for the next birth
Death and wedding.
We carry them
To make us
Real.

He is a teller of tall tales, Talanoa

But what are stories if not lies
Though sweet as vakalolo
Cleaved to our fingers
Floating our souls
In the fat of coconut?

What are memories if not construction:
The storyteller as tattooist
Marking,
And not marking,
Brown skin.

And They say
If your pito-pito is unplanted
       You will wander

They say
If it is unplanted
        Home will elude you

Well mine is buried in story
Planted in a tall tale
And I wander
Yes,
And home is a story
Home is a story where the Frangipani flowers.

VAINE RASMUSSEN

Vaine has published two collections of poems – *Maiata* and *Te Ava-Ora'*. She has recently produced a stage play for the 2010 International Women's Day celebration on Rarotonga. Having worked extensively throughout the Pacific Islands while she was employed by the Secretariat of the Pacific Community as a rural economist, she has enjoyed working in and learning about the many Pacific cultures and people. She resides in Rarotonga and has three sons and a daughter. She has a granddaughter with Ngā Puhi ancestry, for whom this poem was written while she was attending the Takitimu Festival in Heretaunga, Aotearoa. She also has a grandson. Married to Arama Wichman, Vaine writes under her maiden name.

at the Takitimu Festival 2008

well my moko
I'm learning you slowly
your māoridom
your mystical faces
the pōwhiri was a humbling experience
watching the beautiful graceful old women
call me on to the marae at Heretaunga
Mother Maire was there

and Hinemoa
and Tūtānekai
and your King Tuhei
and mine Pa Ariki
and Tamakeu
and our prime minister
and māoridom celebrated
the return of all
parts of the *Tākitimu*
waka
I whispered your name
as I passed rows
and rows of warriors
and maidens
carrying their tūpuna
in their dance
I saw their spirits soar
into the air
and embrace the manuhiri
from near and far

I wish you were here my moko
not because you are māori
but because you are
Tākitimu
because of me.

16/11/08, Leaving Heretaunga

ROSANNA RAYMOND

Of Sāmoan descent, Rosanna Raymond was born in Auckland and now lives in London with her family. Her art practice ranges from installation works, spoken words and body adornment, fusing traditional Pacific practices with modern techniques. She has had residencies at the De Young Museum, San Francisco, the University of Hawai'i at Mānoa and the Cambridge University Museum of Archaeology and Anthropology UK, where she curated the internationally acclaimed *Pasifika Styles* exhibition with Dr Amiria Salmond.

One a Day – a 7 Maiden Rave On
or . . . The Dusky ain't Dead she Just Diversified

Full Tusk Maiden

ex-cannibal, still got a few head-hunting tendencies and sometimes can't tell a predator from the prey . . . oh well they all taste the same. Long of the tooth but still fertile, a red clay lady, been around since the first dawn, introduced Papatūānuku and Nafanua to the Virgin Mary and they have been friends ever since, certainly makes for great ladi nights out. Once had a shark king for a husband but swapped him for a warrior god in the shape of an octopus because he gave better cunnilingus.

Rave on Maiden

that girl can talk, you can't help but listen, her voice is soft and dry like breeze playing with the autumn leaves, she's got skin like the bark of the tree, so often hides in the forest, don't worry if you can't see her as she smells of a 1000 gardenias. Good to have around on long black nights as she is full of myth and magic and has her own sickle moon for you to make a wish on. Loves wearing dog skin, banana flowers and no undies on formal occasions, so don't make her sit cross legged or try to hide her in the rafters.

Hand to Mouth Maiden

a sweet soul ladi, with paua-shell eyes, you can see her back arching across the sky at night, it's swathed in a cloak knitted from glitter, works so hard but always poor . . . keeps her slim though. Will never reveal your secrets, they are safe with her. There's not much to eat up there, so she feasts on rainbows and the odd spaceman when visiting her best friend, Sina, who lives on the moon, you can see them sometimes spitting out the bones. No need for a spacewaka she can fly, but rarely comes to see me, as earthly pleasures are not to her liking.

Hand in Hand Maidens

always ready for some girl on girl action, once they were stuck back to back but were torn apart when they were out playing with some thunder and lightening. Sometimes weighed down by life but loads of sex, good shoes and great friends keep them happy enough, they ain't going to fade to black, because they can chase the clouds away. Has been known to scare the boys so only men need apply to take a peek at their tattooed thighs and hairless vaginas and don't forget to hang on if you go for a ride.

Back Hand Maiden

a ceremonial virgin, with centipede edges, never one for compliments, she's a true savage, quick to bare her buttocks at the slightest offence, has no qualms about slapping your lips and telling you to eat shit, whilst trussing you up like pig ready for the spit . . . but has the most fantastic manners and a loving face with much warmth in her eyes. She had a big black eel for a lover but had him chased away, lest they were discovered, as it would be her own facial blood not that of her hymen she would be covered in.

Fully Laiden Maiden

got big bones and big hair, when she breathes her breasts rise and fall like the swell of the shallow sea, loves wearing mother of pearl and pounamu all at the same time, so she chimes when she walks, always busy so can seem a bit distracted, never the less, a no fuss, no bother, can do sort of a girl. Pretty in a strange sort of a way, you can't help stare at her eyes, they are vast and can light up the night sky, you see she has no pupils, they are vessels containing old gods . . . just don't trip over and fall in them . . . you won't come back alive.

Tu Mucho Maiden

has the meanest huruhuru froufrou you ever did see, thick and dark they look great all oiled up and sprinkled with turmeric, matches her black lips and sunshine smile, loves the feel of leather and feathers and don't pick a fight with her as she knows what to do with a big stick. You should see her on the dance floor, she's got butterfly thighs, you'll want to take her home and introduce her to your mother. Be aware, she needs the salt water to cleanse in, so she can't live far from the sea and make sure she has a soft mat to recline on when indoors, she'll treat you to a song and make you cry.

MOMOE MALIETOA VON REICHE

Born in Sāmoa, Momoe Malietoa von Reiche is a well-known poet, artist, sculptor, photographer, and writer and illustrator of children's books. She runs an art gallery in Sāmoa called M.A.D.D., where she holds periodic performances in dance drama and hosts workshops in creative writing for children.

The Night He Broke My Heart

The night he broke my heart
The moon peeped out of a water-filled sky
Like a mottled sponge ball of inconsequent light.
I cursed that moon for being stand offish
Not sharing the magic that
Once swept me up totally
When I first met him
Under the pinstriped shadows of Matāti'a,
Next to that eerie graveyard by the sea . . .
The moon that night turned the world
Into quasi daylight
When the greens and browns were part
Of one's soul and everything sweet
Fell so completely into place.

Tonight,
Raindrops again cover old moon face
As if obliterating hurts that still
Linger there.
Moon, moon, you are
Still chasing shadows of lovers long gone –
I'm not the only one with
Dreams of you on nights like this
When the moist air filters
Slivers of tempting touches
That lights your soft sensuous
Ageless glow.

The Laugh That Gave Her Away

She has that half
Chinese look
That's deceiving at first
But one could
Almost hear the abacus beads
Clicking and clacking
Inside that compact head
The almond eyes are housed in.
It was behind the white fence
German origin with
Bismarckian scrolls and twists
That I saw her
Sweeping leaves of the vi tree
Freshly fallen yellowed
With August days.
The morning moon hung
Softly steeped in clouds
Like a coconuted breadfruit

I've always wondered what she looked like
This Oriental phenomenon
With a French–English hyphenated name
Vertiginous sounding
Adding mystique to the myth;

The laugh gave her away,
It came out of her stomach
Rather than out of her mouth.
She's Sāmoan by birth.

Pute 'Oso – A Full Life

My mother birthed me
On a sunny day
Biting hard on the umbilical
Which she buried under the nonu tree.
She didn't think twice
But knew that I would succour
Through my earth cord
Like an electrical wire

Revitalising, seeking energy from the goodness
Of the deep earth,
Gaining wisdom from soils of
Whatever has gone before me.

It is the makings of a full life.

REIHANA ROBINSON

Reihana MacDonald Robinson is a poet who lives in the Coromandel. Robinson has worked extensively in the Pacific in arts education, receiving artist residencies at the East-West Center, Hawai'i, and the Anderson Center, Minnesota. She was the inaugural recipient of the Te Atairangikaahu Poetry Award. Her work was included in *AUP New Poets 3* (2008) and she is currently working on a new collection.

Noa Noa Makes Breakfast for Caroline and Me
Or
The Tea Ceremony is Introduced to Sāmoa

The Missionaries. Misguided as usual. Decide *en masse*
To convert the native women
Who are perceived to be holding the purse strings.

So the women observe the missionaries
In their tea drinking. Which includes the refined use
Of what is shaped like a jam spoon.
And is in fact a jam spoon.
Because pikelets must be eaten with the tea.

Never mind the wheat which must be imported
As taro isn't any good for baking pikelets.

So the witnessing begins.
Methodically by Methodists mostly
And it catches.
Only. Who has the teacup?
Who has the saucer?
Who has the precious leaves?

No one woman in the village has
All the utensils or all the ingredients.
Each prizes her own contribution.
And when the tea ceremony is announced
Each woman brings her own offering.

And the cup of tea begins.

So when Caroline's daughter made the ritual 21
Each of Caroline's friends gave her
Gifts of tea. A cup. A spoon.

This long morning we sit in a colonial outpost
And sip our English Breakfast tea
And Noa Noa soon to be 21
Pours tea for Caroline and me.

Waiting for the Pālagi

– I not marry
I free
– The doctor
He safe you life
I luf my boyfren
I luf my Willie
He make luf me
(you no tell anyone)
I luf my Willie
He care for me
He luf me
He care for my boys
Ev'rybody tell me
Leave him
Leave Willie
He no good

Marry the pālagi
But I luf my Willie
Willie he lie me
He has two boys
Many wifes
You know when we at Forgeti's house
All she say
Leave Willie. He no good for you.
Why they tell me that? You know at the market
I see his brother he say
– Willie has two sons
He not lie me
Why Willie make lie?
Tonight I ask Willie

I no want marry the pālagi
My life is suffer
My mind is free.

ETI SA'AGA

Eti Sa'aga was born in Apia, Sāmoa, in 1950. He attended Samoa College and has worked as a heavy equipment driver, translator, planter, journalist/photographer and a radio and television commentator. He has made American Sāmoa his home for the last 30 years, and is currently a United States Congressional staffer. He was married to the late Otilia Hunkin and they have four children, and three grandchildren.

Post Hurricane Observation

In the calm after six days
of the most violent hurricane in decades,
my then two-year-old son looked
at the stripped landscape and said:
        'Daddy! The mountain is all naked!'

I realised what he meant years later
after a bitter divorce from his mother.

Nightfall

Nightfall comes so fast
it pins me on the bed
and drugs me
to a restful sleep.

I swear I can
hear my hair grow.

Outside,
the wind noses
at the wall,
lifts its left hind leg
and splatters on
the concrete and grass
a steady shower
with the golden message:
            'I wuz hea!'

I dream I am
in Heaven sneezing
from the cold of
Nightfall.

Birthday Present

It was the eve
of the new moon
that my daughter
gave me a pebble
for my birthday.
It was gift-wrapped
with tiny fingers,
sticky with mango juice.

LUAFATA SIMANU-KLUTZ

Luafata Simanu-Klutz is a part-time lecturer of Sāmoan language and literature at the University of Hawai'i at Mānoa's Indo-Pacific Languages and Literatures department. She is completing a doctoral degree in history and plans to continue teaching in these fields before she retires. She provides opportunities in her literature courses for students to write poetry and short stories, after reading and discussing works by Sāmoan poets and novelists.

Tinā 'ea

for Tusi

Tinā 'ea . . .
You're seven scores and more.
I should be by your side
to water the wrinkles on your face
and breathe love into your veins
as you did with me
when I was flopping around
on my baby mats.

Tinā 'ea . . .
I should be by your side
to massage youth into your bones
and mend the springs in your feet.
I should be by your side
to lift poverty from your shoulders
and feed you taro and palusami –
and niu for dessert.

Tinā 'ea . . .
When I fly away to perform for others
guilt fills my gut instead of the
lobsters, the size of a ta'amū,
and kina from the reefs of Kusaie,
oozing through my fingers.

Tinā 'ea . . .
Are we destined to be forever apart;
to find life for others who do not care
to say 'Thank you?'

Sau ia 'oe, Tinā.
let us swim again with the tanifa
through the placentas of our foremothers
and taste once more the ingredients of alofa;
and fold into the security of the pe'a
hovering and poising to douse
the fires of prejudice.

CAROLINE (SINA) SINAVAIANA

Caroline Sinavaiana, associate professor of English at the University of Hawai'i at
Mānoa, was born in 1946 on Tutuila island in eastern Sāmoa. Her scholarly
research has been supported by the Ford and Fulbright Foundations, and her
international work in community-based theatre arts has been supported by the
Rockefeller Foundation. She has published two collections of poetry and her
scholarship and creative writing appear in international journals. Her book on
satirical Sāmoan theatre is forthcoming in 2010/11.

In Memoriam: Agnes 'Pako' Yandall Gabbard

Ia manuia lau faigāmalaga
Pako 'Uli: safe journey

1.
To the daughter of Amoa
Where women woo the men.

To the bird from the mountain ridge
That fishes in two seas.

May your wings carry you
To a great nest on the high ridge.

Daughter of the sacred thunder
May her lightning blaze your

Brave path across the night.

2.
Daughter of le ava o i'a eva
Reef channel of the wandering fish

Daughter of le anae oso o fiti
The jumping mullet of Fiji

Daughter of Atua, of Falealili
Of Poutasi, of Nu'u-sa-fe'e

May the sacred octopus jump
Awake in rosy dawn to sweep clear

Your ocean pass.

3.
Daughter of Seinafolava
Daughter of Tuātagaloa

Afio mai lau afioga a Tuatagaloa
'O le to'o savili, 'o le sa'o fetalai.

To the one who guides the boat
Against the wind and gives the first speech:

May Tagaloaalagi of the nine heavens
May Sina and Nafanua

May Iesu Keriso ma lona tinā
Guide your boat against the wind

Into quiet waters of shimmering
Nets & the smoke of cookfires

Rising on the shores of afternoon.

Dear Mom

1.
Now I hear your voice in this
small house by the creek

from that last visit
when you slept on the couch

& prayed the rosary morning
& night, & drank hot water

that last time when I was resting
up between chemo & radiation

when I drove you and Barbara
to the airport but was too sick

to go inside. When a week later
I listened to a phone machine

telling me you were dead.

Now I remember that other house
way back, the one on Willard Road

the first house you ever owned.
Even at 13, I knew the big deal

it was for you. And for me
after the shame of Plew Heights

mine not yours. Where I pretended not
to live when friends' parents dropped

me off after school. Where you worked
nights as a waitress at the NCO Club

to make ends meet. Where Dad worked
nights at Theater No. 1 to make ends meet.

I remember it was 1959, and
there was no grass at the new house.

I remember you planting sprigs of grass,
perfectly straight rows in the front yard.

Now it's 45 years later, & you've been
gone 22 and a ½ months. Now

I think you are somewhere else,
Sāmoa maybe, or the Himalaya.

In your new incarnation
you'll be almost two

the child of parents who prayed
for you to come to them

I think you are the apple of their eyes.
An unusual child, the smartest baby anyone

can remember. I think you will be in
the kitchen, bustling on short legs

or in the cookhouse, organising things
planning dinners for the sandbox

crowd, or village feasts.
I think you will be in the garden

decorating wedding cakes made of mud
teaching the one year olds how

to fashion mud roses for frosting.
I think you will be out front

in the dirt, planting sprigs of grass
in perfectly straight rows.

2.
OK, so Father Sebastian &
the Sacred Heart ladies

beg to differ. *They* see you
in heaven, wearing white tapa

cloth, your designer puletasi
just so.

They see you seated at a small
table next to Jesus, at the ear

of any number of almighties
fund-raising for their next trip

to the Holy Land. They see
you drafting celestial memos

communiqués to Sāmoa, to Bishop X
for example, urging his excellency's

sorry white self to return their
money pronto, while he still has

the chance, while he still has
that difficult-to-obtain precious

human body / while he still has
time to show some respect

for a change / or else /
face the consequences

at the pearly gates where you
his nemesis, now hold sway.

On the other hand, the 50-plus
Birthday Club ladies see you

up there, fund-raising for *their*
pilgrimage to Las Vegas.

They see you up there
rounding up the 80-plus

gals for a birthday luncheon
catered by Auntie Lu's Fish

Grotto, Paradise Branch.
The first in a series of soirées

as long as eternity. You're
holding up a glass of merlot.

You're toasting Reina's mom,
Ida. & your mom, Palepa,

& your sisters, Mary and Lika,
& your cousin Odilla

& Dad's mom, Caroline,
& our Auntie Lu, who stayed

behind just long enough
to make sure we sent you off

in proper style. And so we did.
And so we did.

3.
Auntie Lu. After you left
us, she became you for us.

Organising things. Planning
the lavish feast. Up from her

sickbed to instruct us
your wayward offspring.

Which talking chief gets which
fine mats? of what quality? &

how many? & how many
cases of pisupo? & pilikaki?

& which roast pig? & when?
The gifts flowing back & forth

all night. Speeches flowing back
& forth all night. Lauga. Delegations

of āiga from Savai'i. From 'Upolu.
From Manu'a. From Tutuila.

From Leloaloa, Atuʻu, Pago
Pago, Fagatogo, Fagaʻitua,

Tāfuna, Leone, Malaeʻimi.
Aloʻau, Alofau, Seʻetaga

Nua, Afono, Fāgasā, Tula
Fagaʻitua. From ʻUpolu

Falealili, Poutasi, Apia. From
Savaiʻi. Lano & Puʻapuʻa.

From Hawaiʻi nei. From
Massachusetts, South Carolina

& DC. Speeches flowing
back & forth all night. Lauga.

Words to accompany
you across the sky

words to make a boat
words to make your vaʻa

Sā Tuatagaloa
Sā Seigafo

Sā Falenaoti
Sā Nafanua

Ua pala le maʻa, ua
pala le upu. Stones

pass away, but words
last forever. Carry you

to Pulotu. Carry you to
heaven. Carry you across

the sky.

ALICE TE PUNGA SOMERVILLE

Born in Wellington, Aotearoa New Zealand, in 1975, with primary affiliations to Te Āti Awa, Alice grew up in the Auckland suburb of Glen Innes. After studying at the University of Auckland (MA) and Cornell University (PhD), she returned home to Wellington and lives again on her iwi homelands which are now known as Lower Hutt. She is proud that this makes her Urban Māori both ways. She is a senior lecturer at Victoria University of Wellington, where she teaches in English and Maori studies and researches in the fields of Maori, Pacific and indigenous literary studies. She writes the occasional poem and agrees with Thomas King that 'the truth about stories is that's all we are'.

Daddy's Little Girl

Hours and hours in the back seats of family cars,
long trips and waking up:
snuggled in giant jumpers and sleeping bags,
wrapped in night and stars and sleepy breath.

Dreams and conversations mix, then fade,
and Dad's listening to the radio news:
he's softly clicking and flicking a switch,
a lullaby for young late-night travellers.

Years later when I learned to drive
I was surprised to rediscover the sound
which I'd grown to link with Dad
and sleeping bags and warmth.

An adult now, I drive through the dark,
long long trips wrapped in stars and night:
I think of Dad and his hours of gentle courtesy,
lights dipping and bobbing for passers-by.

feet of clay: a tribute and an accusation

1. cradleboards

you told us about
old people surrounded by death
two hundred years ago
who designed cradleboards
for babies of not-yet-born generations

displayed in museums now
old cradleboards are carefully pinned by amnesia
to the backing paper of timelessness:
the reverse side of treaties and legislation

smaller more portable displays
on postcards and other consumables
for sale at gallery bookshops

what makes death-soaked people quietly embellish a cradle for an unknown baby?

2. a tribute

your carefully tended cradleboards:
balanced and decorated
ready to secure the droopy vulnerable limbs and heads

hunched over a typewriter
you smoothed and reinforced the supple cords
dreamed they would one day knot
around infant shapes of unborn unknown genealogies

what made you gently close the door and lovingly coax a ream of paper to life?

3. a basket

someone else talked about another kind of infant bed
a woven beaded basket
and a baby who slept in her basket until
she was old enough to wake, roll over,
and walk around with it still tied to her back

cruising around the house,
so her father laughed,
like a small turtle

4. an accusation

this week you spoke in ways that shut down space
instead of opening it up

gave people what they wanted to hear
a compromised performance in a soulless place

limbs that had been gently cupped and held
resisted this shifting to another kind of pressure
a diminished constricting: an unwelcome swaddling

you seem to have become
a short-sighted visionary

you weren't supposed to have feet of clay

5. a stone

a large flat stone is set
in the floor of a longhouse
on a campus
on a turtle
for those who need their feet on the ground to speak

this voice shouldn't accuse you
but on the stone on the ground on the turtle
it finds a place to stand:
wearing the basket you yourself wove
a turtle on a turtle
an unknown infant of unexpected genealogy

6. questions

why is it easier for you to lament the forgetting
of cradleboard design

than to recognise your own written cradles
and the revolutionary hope that compelled the act of their creation?

J. C. STURM

Jacquie Sturm was born in Ōpunake, New Zealand, with tribal affiliations to Taranaki iwi, Parihaka and Whakatōhea. She published poetry and short stories in periodicals and anthologies since 1947. In the early 1950s she became the first Māori woman to obtain an MA from a New Zealand university. Sturm's first collection of short stories, *The House of the Talking Cat*), was published in 1983 and her first collection of poems, *Dedications* (1996), received the Honour Award for poetry in the 1997 Montana New Zealand Book Awards. She published a second collection of poems, *Postscripts*, in 2002, and *The Glass House: Stories & Poems* in 2006. Following the death of her husband, James K. Baxter, she worked as a librarian in Wellington for two decades before retiring to Paekākāriki. She died in December 2009 and is buried in her iwi's urupā at Ōpunake.

Spring dreams

With two cats on his lap
a fond woman at his side
(sure she's not a blonde,
can't recall her teens,
but still able enough
and most times willing)

he could be mildly happy.
Mourns instead the life
he thinks he should have had,
wears discontent most days till night,
but then – ah then, realities
he cannot, dare not remember

ambush him in his dreams
demanding to be lived again.

Winter interior

The faded blue couch
keeps on fading
in a weak winter sun.

The old black tomcat
twitches in his young
Bagheera hunting dreams.

The tortoise-shell female
poses like a dancer
on a pyramid in hers.

The old man between them
sinks back thankfully
into sleep, another place,

an earlier time, before
any posing or hunting,
weakening or fading,

before all of these
and me, talking
as usual, to myself.

Disguise

Beware old ladies,
age is their disguise.

Behind that wrinkled mask
a young girl smiles,

her hands still hold
a baby or a lover,

and in her dreams, believes
her prince will surely come.

Request

Lend me your loving
if you cannot give it,
let me lean on your look,
rest my head on your smile.

And later, please not yet,
let me stand in the shadow
of your last going
while my sun goes down.

ROBERT SULLIVAN

Robert Sullivan belongs to the Māori tribes Ngā Puhi (Ngāti Manu / Ngāti Hau)
thanks to his mother; he belongs to Kāi Tahu thanks to his father, who also gifts
him an Irish passport. He has had seven books of poetry published, including
Jazz Waiata and *Star Waka* with AUP, *Cassino City of Martyrs* (2010) with Huia, and
Shout Ha! to the Sky (2010) with Salt Publishing, London. His poetry appears in
Harvard Review, *Berkeley Poetry Review*, *Ploughshares*, *Moving Worlds*, *Salt* and
Landfall. He co-edits the online journal *Trout*, and co-edited with Anne Kennedy
Best New Zealand Poems 2006. His entries on 'Maori Poetry' and 'Polynesian
Poetry' are forthcoming in *The New Princeton Encyclopedia of Poetry and Poetics*.
He served for two years as director of creative writing at the University of
Hawai'i at Mānoa, and is the new head of the creative writing school at Manukau
Institute of Technology.

Captain Cook

Didn't we get rid of him? There are far too many statues, operas
and histories. If only I could be a brown Orwell – a Māori Big Bro,
find every little caption card in every European museum and scrub it out:
change the wording to, 'This was given to Captain Cook as a token of friendship
and should be buried with him', OR 'This was temporarily given to Captain Cook

and would have been expected to be returned on his death', OR 'Well, actually, Captain
Cook stole this', OR 'The Captain exchanged this for something vastly inferior in value – ha
ha for him!' But even as an extra large bro I suspect the lies would leak.
The empire that sent him to his death three times would have its hero.

Māui's Alternate Prayer
with an image from 'Sigh' by Stéphane Mallarmé

Can the sun be drawn out without
                me beating him? Can a yellow
ray soothe the earth like a cool cloth?
                Can the clouds sit on blue a while
  longer? Let them push white over
                the snow-flower mountains draping
    my island, flowers to make leis
                up for the eyes of my waka.
    Let the sun walk gently, longing
                for a good night. Then he can glide.

Took: A Preface to 'The Magpies'

Before we knew what our cousin signed
    for blankets, and grog, we were told in a hui
to move off the land. We wanted to argue
    and kōrero with our arero and puke like the tui

that flew away. The sharp-beaked magpies turned up,
    pecking and squawking, frazzled and screwy.
We tried to unpick the stitches from the new no. 8 wires
    and kōrero'd with our arero and clucked like the tui

that flew away. But it did no good. Our family were not understood.
    Not understood, the farmers said, shooing
us down the dusty trail. Your talk sounds like the magpies –
    all quardling oodling ardling wardling and doodling.

Do you mean to say kōrero, uri, arero, wairua, ruruhau perhaps sir?

Vārua Tupu

for Albert

The equivalent Māori phrase to the Tahitian
is wairua tupu, spirit of growth. Beautiful
beautiful Māʻohi people, tangata whenua.

I see their images in a journal, a photo of Henri Hiro
who calls on the tāngata to write! Write in English!
Write in French! Write in Tahitian! Which
reminds me of Ngũgĩ wa Thiong'o's challenge
to change the world and of Ken Saro-Wiwa's
Ogoni star dancing in the blackness of heaven
and of Haunani-Kay Trask's sharkskin rhythms
calling out Pele in her people and Albert Wendt's
spiralling caul of liquid fire.

We connect ourselves with poems of struggle,
hearts hammering like Martín Espada's father,
fear embraced and set free by Joy Harjo. I serve
Cervantes. He sat down on his back step
near 60, one-armed, two whole teeth in his head,
and began to write *Don Quixote* said W. S. Merwin
as he began a reading here. Allen Curnow
recited to me 'I the poet William Yeats'
and Robert Kroetsch read with the heart
of a young man, while Margaret Atwood's eros
poems rested their wings with me. Write out the lives,
write them alive, write till the fire strikes,
another fire, a torch, a whakaaraara warning cry
kia hiwa rā! kia hiwa rā! kia hiwa rā ki tēnei tuku!
kia hiwa rā ki tēnā tuku!* Watch every terrace
of the fortress, there's an enemy climbing up,
a blaze from heaven, kia hiwa rā! my friend.

So I light a fire here in this stanza,
my small room with large windows,
carried from the fires on the hills
and the haka fires in the poets
from the processions of mysteries
and lamped freeways, from history sourced
in gin of the Fleet Ditch and Gordon Riots,

---

* Be alert! Be alert! Be alert at this terrace! Be alert at that terrace!

and James Cook's golden narratives
to our own kōrero neherā, our oral
bodies caressed tuku iho tuku iho down
to present hands cupped to mouths
as we plunge and rise in the ancestor ocean
shield our eyes from bullet-train rays
and think of our father Māui
who planted himself and his brothers
in the East who caught Tamanui the Sun
after the night at the crater
of the creator our mother the Earth.

Poet Henri Hiro in brotherly spirit I embrace you.
Je t'embrasse. Ka awhi au i a koe e te tuakana.
Moe mai moe mai moe mai rā e te tama manawawera,
te tama ngākau mārie hoki. He waiata aroha,
he mihi mīharo nā te kitenga o ō waiata, ō whakaaro
painga mō ngā tāngata moutere. Ka haka!
I turn back to the flame of life. Ka oriori au: tihei mauri ora!*

Fragments of a Māori Odyssey

i Laertes' Shroud

I've been weaving this for years,
trying to make a cloak fit for a chief in state,
warding off the newcomers until
our sovereignty returns.

ii Bow

The proverb says never to bow your head
unless it's to a mighty range of mountains.
Another proverb says that a man will die for two
things: Women and land. Parts of me have already
died for these but I am ready to pass
my fingers through a needle to reach them.

---

* I embrace you. I hug you older brother. Rest here, sleep here
hot-hearted son, son of peace. A song of love,
an astonished greeting at the sight of your songs,
your blessed thoughts for island peoples. I haka!
I turn back to the flame of life. I chant the breath of life!

iii Sea

The cyclops have written their critiques,
some so harsh it's hard to cross the sea
feeling easy, assured of a welcome home.
The portents for a return are wrong.

iv Ithaca

Hawaiki ends the longing, where the soul
rests after its dive to the beloved.
We enter the great house baring our feet
and those of us who believe put on wings.

Cape Return
for Alistair Te Ariki Campbell

Carried out by tears, songs and speeches
they make offerings on their journeys –
the atua are strange, 'plant gods, tree gods',
who'd strike them – until the familiar
path shudders down – a heavy wave

on the shining sands of the longest beach.
Spirits flying from east and west, ridging
the spine between, meet at the headland
above Tōhē's beach. At Maringi Noa
they look back, tears thundering down to join

new ones coming north. At Waingunguru
the stream mourns them. They climb another hill,
reach another stream – then a waterfall
silenced by their crossing. They continue
the last ascent, a ridge, which lifts up the cape

to Hiriki, then a sharp fall where water
lies waiting to hold them. They are expected
to drink and swallow the night, with
a chance, even then, to stay – the sentinel
there has the power to turn them back.

They continue. Desires splutter like spit
on flames. They're leaving for long Hawaiki,
to sail, dip and chant like birds forever.
The mist swarms over the last cliff, climbs off
the last piece of coast over the ocean, home.

Ahi Kā – The House of Ngā Puhi

We light the poem and breathe out
          the growing flames. Ahi kā. This
                    is our home – our fire. Hot tongues out

– pūkana – turn words to steam. This
          fish heart is a great lake on a
                    skillet. Ahi kā! Ahi kā!

Keep the fire. The sun's rays are ropes
          held down by Māui's brothers.
                    They handed down ray by burning

ray to each other every
          day – we keep the home fires burning
                    every day. Mountains of our

house are its pillars – I believe
          in the forces that raised them here.
                    Ahi kā burnt on to summits

char in the land, ahi kā dream,
          long bright cloud brilliant homeland.
                    Ahi kā our life, ahi kā

carried by the tribe's forever-story
          firing every lullaby.
                    Shadows shrink in our hands' quiver

as we speak – ahi kā sing fire
          scoop embers in the childhood sun
                    stare into molten shapes and see

people – building, sailing, farming –
          see them in the flames of our land
                    see them in this forever light

no tears only fire for ahi
 kā no weeping only hāngī pits
no regrets just forgiveness and

a place for the fire – its our song
to sing – ahi kā – got to keep
singing the shadows away – ha!

SAGE TAKEHIRO

Sage Uʻilani Takehiro was born in Hilo, Hawaiʻi, in 1982. She has won several writing awards, including the Ernest Hemingway Award for poetry from the University of Hawaiʻi. Her first collection of poetry, *Honua*, was published by Kahuaomanoa Press. She has worked as a columnist for the *Big Island Weekly*, and for the University of Hawaiʻi in the development of culture-based language arts curricula.

Kou Lei

I was a fetal spirit born in the ti-leaf womb of our mother
You uncurled my body and saw severed stems of white ginger
layered over each other
ʻawapuhi keʻokeʻo standing side by side
braided tightly in fine fibres, woven
into rope by loving hands
that dangled
on each end

You pressed your nose against me
kissed my fragrance
and opened your eyes as you returned your breath

You held me in my ti leaf cradle, saw the brown footprints of rain
and ʻAʻala Honua that blows through the strands of your hair

You knew that I slept on a bed of ginger roots
                    drizzled with dirt

    You watched my petals unfold and twist
        eyes of white ginger
            jumbled into my wrists as I rubbed them, crying
    for Honua to feed my flowers
                while forbidden blossoms were held firm
            in the rope bones of my body

            You peeled me from the ti-leaf and held me against your chest
I wrapped my arms around you and you tied my hands behind your
                    neck
            my mana
            carried by yours

        I lay on top of your shoulders
                    listening to our life beat
                        through your skin

    You wear my beauty
            while I breathe yours

            I am your lei

An Artist's First Friday

Adorned in lei pīkake, she converses among black stars.
He stands, hand in pocket, hand holding drink,
lei are stink to him, but she smells sweet.

He writes her a poem, draws it in the air with his
pointer finger. They stand against the Ko'olau,
those mountain ridges that dream of Kaua'i, an ancestor.

Onlookers feel oceans in their veins –
pulls pores out of their skin, like gold rain
on black canvas. Night falls

makes love with the light, makes mountains
glassy, makes mist steam in black moonlight.
Dreams of Kanaka cousins stretch

to the end of the world
where a court of Gods pierce pictures
with graceful urgency –

like the blood-red memories
of Halema'uma'u. Pele's pit opens
with a maile lei that welcomes death.

Fire burns through the pen of a poet
filled with red ink, flows like lava on a book of photographs,
while its author paints acrylic imagery, and smells the lei pīkake.

Hina-i-ke-ahi

Fire-bread. Ulu. Less.
Famine on the land.

She comes
arising from the salty sea
adorned with a lengthy lei
of limu, crawls on to the lava rocks

raped of pūpū, ko'ako'a, and
aquarium fish. She stands

naked, reaches to where the moon
retires to the horizon
and pulls from it
a sheet of kapa –
fabric ripples over the ocean.
She wraps herself,
and inches inland.

She wakes the women,
with her moonflower breath
and the men, she awakes
by arousing the sun,

E ala e, she chants, eh,
no get nuts, because
you hungry. Eh, for real.
Dig a puka into our mother,

fashion a fire inside of it,
and set the rocks as a foundation.

She descends into the pit
wrapped in kapa, pressed
on top, with kukui ink and 'ohe,
are banana leaves.
                    Leave me
here for three days, she told the women,
the men, and the children, who dug
and carried rock, and fashioned fire
for this pit.

They smell the smoking ulu, the food to feed
the famine, the flesh of a goddess.

When the third day arrives
they plough their fingers
through piles of dirt, peel
the banana leaves from her kapa
find the pit full with fire-bread.

A keiki takes his ulu to the shore
to share with his friends, the pūpū,
the ko'a, and the aquarium fish,
there he sees her walking naked
into waves, he waves, a hui hou,

Hina-i-ke-ahi

TRACEY TAWHIAO

Tracey Tawhiao is a writer, poet, film-maker, lawyer and visual artist. She has iwi links to Ngāi Te Rangi from Matakana Island and Tūwharetoa, Taumarunui, as well as Whakatōhea. After receiving a law degree and BA in classical studies, Tawhiao began practising as an artist. Her writing has been widely published in magazines and journals and her paintings and poetry featured in the book *Taiawhio* (Te Papa Press, 2006). She is the head of Artist & Repertoire for music management company Heartmusic. She is also a director of The House of Taonga, a Maori artist house of thought and creative endeavour.

My Mother and Me

I'm sweeping my kitchen floor
Then I make the beds
I clean the toilets
I wash the dishes
I wipe down the bench

My mother says I'm a bit slack with my cleaning

I'm bathing my kids
I warm their pajamas in the hot-water cupboard
I get mad because they are moaning
I get their towels off the heater
I dress them

My mother says I don't get right into the corners

I'm writing a poem
Then I fill in my diary
I hang up a painting
I flick through a novel
I find my page
I'm in bed

My mother says your poems are so angry can't you write nice things

I'm dreaming and I wake crying
I start writing
When I was small I coloured in
I get up when it's light
I make the kids breakfast
I pack them a lunch

My mother says be nicer to your husband, he's a good man

I'm starting my day again
Sweeping the floor
Making the beds
Writing a poem
Running a bath
Cooking a meal

My mother says I don't have one single memory of playing with you
Isn't that awful, I don't think I ever played with you.

APIRANA TAYLOR

Born in New Zealand, Apirana Taylor is of Ngāti Porou, Te Whānau ā Apanui, Ngāti Ruanui and Ngāti Pākehā descent. He is a poet, novelist, short-story writer, playwright, actor and painter, who tries to earn a living as a freelance artist, but currently teaches creative writing at Whitireia Polytechnic. Apirana has won awards for his poetry and drama and is currently working on a manuscript of two of his plays to be published by Pohutukawa Press. His publications include five books of poetry, most recently *Te Ata Kura: The Red-tipped Dawn* (2003) and *A Canoe in Midstream* (2009), both published by Canterbury University Press; two books of short stories, *He Rau Aroha* and *Ki Te Ao*; and one novel, *He Tangi Aroha*. He has been the writer in residence at Massey University and Canterbury University, and he has toured Europe reading his poetry, which has also been translated into German.

tangiwai

tangiwai weeping water
weeping water tangi
water tangi weeping
tangi weeping wai
weeping wai water
wai water weeping
water weeping waitangi
weeping waitangi tangiwai
waitangi tangiwai weeping

jetty in the night

slap suck slap suck
slap slap suck waves lap
slap slap lap lap
around the jetty
in the night

zigzag roads

roads in Taranaki
zigzag and snake their way
over the bitter earth
they seldom run straight

roadmakers
paid compensation
only when they ran the roads
through Pākehā land

they didn't pay
if they pushed their roads
through the tattered remnants
of Māori land

hence roads crazily
snake and zigzag
through the province

the liars' road
is never straight

fishbone

how it must've stuck in their gullets like a fishbone
to have their plans foiled by a black little one-eyed
monkey called Tītokowaru

he could count his fighting warriors
on his fingers and toes
if he counted old women and children

Cameron gutted Taranaki
opened it up like a can of beans

he knew the cause was unjust

in search of honour glory riches and fame
they came Whitmore, McDonnell, von Tempsky
the Kai Iwi cavalry

their dreams lie buried on the battlefield

a bullet shot von Tempsky

he got a street named after him

Maxwell, his sabre thirsting for the blood of more
children, was shot on his horse charging again

blood and butchery

Whitmore, McDonnell, got hollow victory
meaningless medals empty fame

Tītoko's army, old men, women, warriors and children,
unbeaten, melted away, a fight over a woman they say
breaking of tapu

eat the rocks, chew and choke on the bones

sings Tītokowaru jailed in his cave

Hinemoa's daughter

her hair is so long
you could plait it all the way to the moon
and weave it with a sprinkling of stars

she writes poetry
as only the muse can write

when she smiles
she melts the heart of God

'I'm from Te Arawa,' she says
she shows me her litany of scars
they climb like ladders
up the insides of her wrists

deep savage cuts to the bone
speak of her youth and the countless times
she sent herself along the path of the spirits
and sought the solace of Hine-nui-te-pō

like her tipuna Hinemoa
she swam the lake
but her lake was of fire and death
broken bottles drunken fights
smashed families shattered and scattered whānau

and she made it
she crossed the troubled water
and found her tāne who loves her
more deeply then the heart can tell

in the lost city
they raise many fine children
with aroha

KONAI HELU THAMAN

Born and raised in Tonga, Konai Helu Thaman was educated both there and in New Zealand, where she gained her BA in geography at the University of Auckland and trained as a teacher. She taught high school in Tonga before going on to further study: gaining her MA in international education from the University of California in 1974 and in 1988 a PhD from the University of the South Pacific, where she has lectured ever since. There Konai has been director of the Institute of Education, head of the School of Humanities and pro vice-chancellor. She currently holds a personal Chair in Pacific Education and Culture and a UNESCO Chair in Teacher Education and Culture. Konai has published five collections of poetry: *You, the Choice of My Parents* (1974), *Langakali* (1981), *Hingano* (1987), *Kakala* (1993) and *Songs of Love* (1999), had one collection translated into German (*Inselfur*, 1987) and her work is studied in schools throughout the Pacific. Konai is married with two adult children.

peace
for Adam Curle

today we come together
to read and sing of peace
lay aside our differences

rise and greet the breeze
there's no need to explain
define or defend our theme
question our ancestors
about their silent dreams
no need to blame the rain or pain
for crying on the phone
no need to ask how far the tide
will come and meet our bones

when all is said and done
you'll have to give up soon
the things that make you what you are
the things you think you own
a spouse a house
a child a friend
the land your customs
even the pain
for when you're left with nothing
only wings to lift you up
you'll see how fast your soul is trembling
freedom trapped in a cup
seize it now hold it tight
have no fear you're there
let me whisper no I'll shout
peace is in the air

the way ahead

we cannot see
far into the distance
neither can we see
what used to stand there
but today we can see
trees separated by wind and air
and if we dare to look
beneath the soil
we will find roots reaching out
for each other
and in their silent intertwining
create the landscape
of the future

letter to feifafa

dear feifaia
i have your picture
on my wall
just above the light switch

your face
a mixture of joy and sadness
weaving hope and anxiety
into a royal garland
a story-line traces
our origins
among bitter-sweet messages
of old

it hurts me
to remember
how she went to be offered
back to the land
how you helped her
to live and die
how you tried to see
her beauty in death
green radiance
of a forgettable dawn

how many times
have you died
from tattooed hands that torture
and countless unseen wounds
opening through nodes
that connect our sorrows
to the harsh strokes
of society

tear-stained tapa
soaked in blood
continue to flow
from the over-filled kava bowl
of our rulers
their quick acceptance
of your sacrifice
still bleeds

at the cutting edge
of time

i have been thinking
over what you did
that dark day long ago
i still don't believe
that a king was worth it!

letter to the colonel

sir some people are sad
because of your words
and actions
that is why i bring you
this cup of kava
from your neighbour's soil

it contains the tears
of workers, farmers, miners
fisherfolk who go down
to the depths of adopted
seas for food
many have lost their jobs
robbed of opportunities
to make a profit
here, take it anyway
symbol of suffering and sorrow
of women

in the fields
in garment factories
at home where children
cry out their fears and frustration
take it, sir, it is yours

ah, but you see, sir
for some this cup is full
of hope
when you drink it you
will know your victory
like the kava it comes

from the roots
of people's hopes in the land
their collective confidence
will lift you up
their new-found pride
will bloom around you
while they wait
for their duty-bound son
to bury his weapons
and liberate their souls

and by the way, sir
i hope that as you drink this
you will remember
that when the dawn breaks
no one can shut out
the light

HELEN TIONISIO

Helen Tionisio is a poet of Sāmoan and Tokelauan descent. Born and raised in Petone, Wellington, she graduated with an arts degree from Victoria University and now continues her work as a poet/spoken word artiste in Auckland. This poem is based on her two months' experience in Sāmoa looking after her Tokelauan grandfather, Tioni Pasilio, while he was undergoing major surgery. Helen writes, *Sāmoa helped me laugh awhile during some very trying times.*

Sāmoa

Sinamoga Saanapu Leififi and Lelata
These are villages I can call my own

Many a times I walked amongst banana trees
And greenery with Papa Tioni
Felt the deep soft grass underneath my dusty feet

Walked to that shop Lynn's down the road
For sanity: ice cream, donuts, apples, vaiola and Oreos

Had a 20-tala haircut from this New Zealand Sāmoan guy
Who moved from West Auckland to the great surf that is Sāmoa
Ah, Sāmoa
12-tala burgers and churches next door
To housie and bingo and apa i'a galore

5-tala movies at Magik Cinemas
Yeah right magik,
So magik, that they don't give refunds if the power goes off in the
middle of movies
*No, the power has to go off three times and then you can have your
money back*

And if the power did go off
Someone has crashed into a power pole – again!
Auoia
Piula
Was Peeutiful
And those steps down to the cave pool were
Huge
Like Mt Fusi
Rocksteady and Big and Glorious
Vi'ia le Atua mo Sāmoa e
(Sa'o lelei)

22009 – *Can I have a taxi to Lelata? fa' amolemole
le fale o Maka*
Le Tala Fou with Verona Parker
Lunch at Gourmet Seafoods
Where Aunty Tia works with her daughter

And you can't forget Otto/Auto Supacentre
Pat AhHim's and the makeki
Chan Mow and the specials on apa supakeki
And the screams from the old plantation non stop
Yeah Kapisi – I thought of you on my way down from Faleolo

Walking the streets of Apia
Ignoring wolf whistles and car horns beeping – or trying to beep
The looks my pālagi skin gets when I walk into chemists
*You're not from here
You shouldn't be here*

– if only you could read my mind . . . beep, beebeebeep beep beep

My name is Helen Tionisio
And I have pālagi skin

I survived 2 months in Sāmoa
With my pālagi skin
Short black hair
Single
No kids

Sāmoa
4 and a half hours away
From Niu Sila
1 and a half days
By boat to Tokelau

Sāmoa
Where I constantly thought
Of my faraway places

Constantly questioned my Sāmoa e
Constantly refused to catch buses so waved down taxis to get around

Where taxis are these flashy bombs
With the mirrors, eagles, flags and radios on
Where taxi drivers went out of their way
For their customers – for the 2 tala they pay
Playing dumb after hearing my pālagi accent
Even if I was playing dumb when they were asking
You kedda poyfren?
A'e,
If only you could read my mind (God get me outta here!)
If only this car door would open from the inside!
Fobby taxis and fobby taxi driver
Opens the door see, from the outsider
Apia to Lelata in the taxi *ka'a*
Ahh, Sāmoa e
Where 2 tala takes you *fa'a*

BLAINE TOLENTINO

Blaine Tolentino was born on a very full moon in 1987 and raised in Kailua and Ko'olina on O'ahu in Hawai'i. She graduated with a bachelors degree in English from the University of Hawai'i at Mānoa in 2009. Under the name 'societyofanimals', Blaine blogs poetry and occasional recommendations of art, books and music.

Patsy Cline/Genesis

The assertion of echoes
on Catholic school nuns
is as such: as the peacock
drags, tarnishes its lovely
tail on earth, so bundles
up priesthoods of rules
and riddles to crack and tarnish
the wet skin of heathens
in fourth grade.

My father drove me to school,
because my mother was lousy
with a depression (brought on
by AIDS death of uncles
and friends). She fell asleep
when the sun came up, when
I packed up my last spelling bee
and wrestled milk toward
the stomach and anonymous bowels
that existed and pumped and erred
but couldn't be seen, so might as well
have been a machine with small
friends pumping cogs on wheels.

On the way, my father played
Patsy Cline from a tape that was stuck
in the mouth of the car's body –
my cousin was there, in a matching

red plaid, starched and criss-crossed
on strappy backs – she could prove
this all happened, if called upon.

We fought the repertoire for a long
while, forming political opinions
on old music and continual discontent
– we would not be silenced.
After a while, though, because
the songs were the only thing we heard,
we knew all the words and all
of the bad things she felt about
men with cars and other women
and how everything would hurt us.

Shiva's Left and Right Shoulder and Hand

Delinquents of the night, they shuttered and swayed
on my front porch with purple Jesus, grape juice
and vodka in a mason jar singing. Swing the quartz
grasp and glow.

Delinquents of the night, they painted and prayed
my face into Aztecs and Mayans battling across my eyes
and into the dark night, on that bridge by the graveyard,
on that staircase of hobos and travelling musicians.

Delinquents of the night, they haunted and harrowed
each other from separate rooms, birdcall disaster
and grasping the handle to jump out and scare
bystanders, beautiful virgins right out of their clothes.

Delinquents of the night, they tremble and tumble
themselves into bed, easing the ache of wild highs
and chasing thunder around the apartment with tomahawks.
Feverous feuds could go on toward the morning
infinitely.

HAUNANI-KAY TRASK

Haunani-Kay Trask is a writer, scholar, speaker, indigenous leader and human rights organiser. Trask holds a PhD degree in political science from the University of Wisconsin. She is professor of Hawaiian studies at the University of Hawai'i, and served for ten years as the director of the University of Hawai'i's Center for Hawaiian Studies. She is also one of the founders and leading members of Ka Lāhui Hawai'i, the largest native sovereignty organisation in Hawai'i. She has represented Hawai'i's indigenous people at the United Nations Working Group on Indigenous Peoples in Geneva, and at numerous indigenous gatherings across the world. She has published many articles on the struggle for self-determination of Hawai'i's indigenous people, books including *From a Native Daughter: Colonialism and Sovereignty in Hawai'i* and the collections of poetry, *Light in the Crevice Never Seen* and *Night is a Sharkskin Drum*. She also served as a scriptwriter and co-producer of the award-winning documentary film *Act of War: The Overthrow of the Hawaiian Nation*.

Nā 'Ōiwi

I

How is it
    your black Hawaiian hair,
        flowing in red-tipped waves,
            a cloak of fine, burnt feathers

from our ancient past,
    now rests on white
        coffin folds, false satin
            finish in the gloss,

as if our people couldn't
    tell by their touch
        the undertaker's hand, as if
            the gleam of your magnificent

time could be muted
　　　　by the waxy smell
　　　　　　　of missionary lies.

II

How is it now
　　　　you are gone,
　　　　　　　our ali'i dismembered,
　　　　　　　　　　their mana lost,
we are left
　　　　with broken bodies, blinded
　　　　　　　children, infected winds
　　　　　　　　　　from across the sea.

How is it,
　　　　our bones cry out
　　　　　　　in their infinite dying,
　　　　　　　　　　the haole and their ways

　　　　　　　　　　　　have come to stay.

Nāmakaokaha'i

Born from the chest
　　　　of Haumea, mo'o
　　　　　　　woman of kuapā,
　　　　lizard-tongued goddess
　　　　　　　of Hawai'i:
　　　　　　　　　　Nāmakaokaha'i,
　　　　　　　　　　　　sister of thunder
　　　　　　　and shark –
　　　　　　　　　　Kānehekili,
　　　　　　　　　　　　Kūhaimoana
　　　　　　　elder of Pele,
　　　　　　　　　　Pelehonuamea.

Kino lau on the wind,
　　　　　　in the yellowing ti,
　　　　　　　　sounds of Akua
　　　　　　　　　　awaking in the dawn:

— 234 —

Nā-maka-o-ka-haʻi,
eyes flecked with fire,
summoning her family

from across the seas.

Sharks in the shallows,
upheaval in the heavens.

From the red rising mist
of Kahiki, the Woman of the Pit:

Pele, Peleʻaihonua,
travelling the uplands,

devouring the foreigner.

Where the Fern Clings

where the fern
clings, lingering
above slit

rock, shadows
musky in hot
perfume

. . . the cries
of tight-winged birds

flickering tongues,
damplit skin,

the seep
of summer
thirst

In Our Time

in memory of Noa Tong Aluli, Hawaiian of the land, 1919–1980

today, I went to the grave
no flowers, no tears, no words

the wind came up slightly
from the ocean
salt and warmth

you were the earth
as you are now

I cannot imagine
your life, being
younger by a generation:
all those children, all
that work, so much silence

in the end, your going
was familiar: a family
trial, burning nightly

certain to the bitter end
your sons, your wife
your daughter
myself

and now, there is
only earth, the salt
wind, a small
story of many years

I came to understand
but only the sea remains
constant and dark

O Noa, we don't
live like you anymore
there is nothing
certain in this world

except loss
for our people

and a silent grief,
grieving

Chant of Lamentation

I lament the abandoned
terraces, their shattered
waters, silent ears
of stone and light

    who comes trailing
    winds through
    taro loʻi?

I lament the wounded
skies, unnourished
desolate, fallen drunk
over the iron sea

    who chants
    the hollow ipu
    into the night?

I lament the black
and naked past, a million ghosts
laid out across the ocean floor

    who journeys from
    the rising to the setting
    of the sun?

I lament the flowers
ʻaʻole pua, without
issue on the stained
and dying earth

    who parts the trembling
    legs, enters where
    the god enters, not
    as a man but as a god?

I lament my own
long, furious lamentation
flung down
into the bitter stomachs

into the blood-filled streams
into the far
and scattered graves

> who tells of those
> disinterred, their
> ground-up bones, their
> poisoned eyes?

Sisters
for Mililani

I
doves in the rain

mornings above
Kāne'ohe Bay   blue
sheen stillness
across long waters gliding
to Coconut Island

channels of sound
color   rhythmic
currents   shell
picking   jellyfish
hunting   squeals
of mischief oblivious
in the calm

II
rain pours
steady   clouding
the light   dark
mornings   darker
evenings   silted
in the night   smell of dead

fish   dead
limu   dead
reef

eight million
for Coconut Island
five hundred thousand
for townhouses
on the hill   traffic
and greedy foreigners
by the mile

III
destruction as a way
of life   clever
haole culture
killing as it goes

'no stone
left unturned'
no people
left untouched

IV
in every native
place   a pair
of sisters
driven by the sound
of doves

the color of
morning

defending life
with the spear
of memory

Colonisation

I
Our own people
say, 'Hawaiian
at heart.' Makes
me sick to hear

how easily
genealogy flows
away. Two thousand
years of wise

creation bestowed
for a smile
on resident non
natives.

'Form of survival,'
this thoughtless inclusion.
Taking in
foreigners and friends.

Dismissing history
with a servant's
grin.

II
Hawaiian at heart:

nothing said
about loss
violence, death
by hundreds of thousands.

Hawaiian at heart:

a whole people
accustomed
to prostitution
selling identity

for nickels
and dimes
in the whorehouses
of tourism.

III
Hawaiian at heart:
why no 'Japanese
at heart?'

How about
'haole at heart?'

Ruling classes
living off
natives

first
land

then
women

now
hearts

cut out
by our own
familiar hand.

HONE TUWHARE

Born in Kaikohe in 1922, Hone Tuwhare (Ngā Puhi) was New Zealand's most distinguished Maori poet writing in English. His first poetry collection, *No Ordinary Sun*, was published in 1964 and his following books of poetry include *Selected Poems* (1980), *Year of the Dog: Poems New and Selected* (1982), *Mihi: Collected Poems* (1987), *Deep River Talk* (1993), *Shape-Shifter* (1997), *Piggy Back Moon* (2001) and *Oooooo......!!!* (2005). He was the Burns Fellows in 1974, the University of Auckland's Literary Fellow in 1991 and Te Mata Poet Laureate in 1999–2000; won two Montana New Zealand Book Awards; and held two honorary doctorates in literature. In 2003 he was among ten of New Zealand's greatest living artists named as Arts Foundation of New Zealand Icon Artists. Tuwhare passed away in 2008.

Kereihi ('Standing quite still')

Standing quite still we stare out
     over the City through the upstairs windows
     of your townhouse: we were twin spoons, back
     to front, or, just lumped together under
     a stretched jersey buttoned up.

     Over your left shoulder my eyes traced
     the forgotten lineaments of Rangitoto, the white
     harbour lying somnolent in the moonlight.

But my eyes are second guessing:
     they're withdrawn. It's the memory of clearer
     sightings of you and the City that is pushing
     the moonbeams aside . . .
     You have Presence, elan. Townhouse, and now
     here . . . at Tomarata, where the stars at night
     bully and make swollen the ocean – and me meek.

     You're all around me – matt bordered
     framed or unframed, the pictures on canvas,
     on paper, staring out of the walls give an
     exuberant feel of people, cats, cars, a huge

sword that would take two hands to wield, the
slender arms of the harbour drenched with
colour, beckoning . . . Well, I love the

unostentatious, rough-sawn roofbeams of your house;
exposed, unabashed, and under which I have snored
and snored without causing any structural damage.
. . . At risk of being presumptuous, it must be said:
and I say it

because it seems absolutely right to retain
the smallest hope that you too may remember the sun
and sum of my embraces, without ever knowing that
there were times when memories such, bestow a thin
moon of wretchedness – an abyssmal affliction
of torment of emptiness – to my arms to my hands
to my lips: Kereihi

The backbone of things

I look skew-whiff at the way
        you shape your feelings through
        your fingers, your brushes;
        the angular swish of arms
        and hips as you address
        the canvas – your eye
        checking the plumb-line for
        the lie of the face or of
        the land, with your hand
        held out at arm's length
        like a slim axe and
        I wonder what next as
        I sit for you eyes akimbo
        my arms held stiffly down
        my sides, my piles beginning
        to give me arseholes.

        and I think, oh boy, thus
        far for me & no further:
        then you lay your brushes
        down and you invite me
        to have a look. I look.

It is a dark summary of all
    my joyful sins and I
    don't say nothing for a minute:

    maybe we could proscribe
    each other by placing
    the result of each one's
    recent *ouvrage* side by side
    to make a two-pager –
    a tiny book together –
    a love story full of storm
    and tears – full of storm
    and tears and love –
                but mostly love. Always

Ode to a blowfly

I see you maggot,
cuddled around
a spear of grass
growing from a mere
jumble of now-fleshless
bones – the left-overs
of a sumptuous feast. Soon
your body will change
your wings glisten &
dry, and as you
draw strength from
the Sun; check the
pads on your feet
take flight & buzz
the odours of a rich
man's kitchen or the
weeping sores of the
poor. Your nose has
identified the strength
& density of smell
of each target. The
wild uncontrolled sound
of your buzzing indicates
how maddening it is
to make a choice.

It is also a signal to your kin
to shake off the blind torpors of the maggot-life,
for a life-style defying gravity & with
padded feet crawl over and around carrion
flesh savouring their taste & smell with infinite
      delicacy, leisurely, again, again, you wipe
    your feet on food before it reaches a human mouth.

On becoming an Icon (!)

Except for a couple absentee
      Icons, together, we stand –
      all ten of us comically sardonical;
      sartorially
      succeeding only in being
      dark-suited –
      bow-tied & white-shirted,
      but secretly stretched
      in bowel and
      bladder control, as

the Governor-General,
      Dame Silvia, pins
      a round, green-stoned-
      cored badge, on our
      plumped-up chests to a series
      of comically repressed 'Ow-ouches'
      and discovering politically that
      we are all 'Lefties'
      as the pin lances
      a left nipple.

We become more phylosophically
      dead in the face, as
      our lips curl to a
      comically heroic, tightlipped
      silence of
      painful acceptance,
      laconically iconical!

To Elespie, Ian & their Holy Whānau

On life's eternal river
     we float on . . . and
     on, forever – like
     a stream of light
     enhancing our understanding
     of human love,
     and life! Kia ora!

'I feel like a vulnerable pā-site'

I feel like a vulnerable
     pā-site, sacked, by
     an unforgiving enemy
     force & razed to a level
     unbecoming, to a warrior-force,
     but – freed at last,
     to accept – with humility –
     the earth-smelling pungency
     of that Grand Dame – mother,
     of us all: Papa-tū-ā-Nuku:
     our Earth-mum.

ALBERT WENDT

Albert Wendt is of the āiga Sa-Maualaivao of Malie, the āiga Sa-Su'ā of Lefaga, the āiga Sa-Malietoā of Sapapaali'i, and the āiga Sa-Pātū and Sa-Asī of Vaiala and Moata'a, Sāmoa. Novelist, poet, short-story writer, playwright and academic, he has been an influential figure in the developments that have shaped New Zealand and Pacific literature since the 1970s. He is the author of seven novels, four books of short stories, four collections of poetry, three plays, a history of the early years of the Mau movement in Sāmoa, seminal essays and articles on Pacific writing and art, and the editor of four major anthologies of Pacific writing. His work has been translated into many languages and is taught around the world. He is now emeritus professor at the University of Auckland. He and his partner, Reina Whaitiri, have eight mokopuna.

The Ko'olau

1.

Since we moved into Mānoa I've not wanted to escape
the Ko'olau at the head of the valley
They rise as high as atua as profound as their bodies
They've been here since Pele fished these fecund islands
out of Her fire and gifted them the songs
of birth and lamentation

Every day I stand on our front veranda
and   on acid-free paper   try and catch their constant changing
as the sun tattoos its face across their backs

Some mornings they turn into tongue-
less mist my pencil can't voice or map
Some afternoons they swallow the dark rain
and dare me to record that on the page

What happens to them on a still and cloudless day?
Will I be able to sight Pele Who made them?
If I reach up into the sky's head will I be able
to pull out the Ko'olau's incendiary genealogy?

At night when I'm not alert they grow long limbs
and crawl down the slopes of my dreams and out
over the front veranda to the frightened stars

Yesterday Noel   our neighbour's nine-
year-old son   came for the third day
and watched me drawing the Ko'olau
Don't you get bored doing *that*? he asked
Not if your life depended on it! I replied
And realised I meant it

2.

There are other mountains in my life:
      Vaea who turned to weeping stone as he waited
for his beloved Apaula to return   and who now props
up the fading legend of Stevenson to his 'wide and starry sky'
and reality-TV tourists hunting for treasure islands

      Mauga-o-Fetu near the Fafā at Tufutafoe
at the end of the world where meticulous priests gathered
to unravel sunsets and the flights of stars that determine
our paths to Pulotu or into the unexplored
geography of the agaga

Taranaki Who witnessed Te Whiti's fearless stand at Parihaka
against the settlers' avaricious laws and guns
Who watched them being evicted and driven eventually
from their succulent lands but not from the defiant struggle
their descendants continue today   forever until victory

3.

The Ko'olau watched the first people settle in the valley
The Kanaka Maoli planted their ancestor   the Kalo
in the mud of the stream and swamps
and later in the terraced lo'i they constructed
Their ancestor fed on the valley's black blood
They fed on the ancestor
and flourished for generations

Recently their heiau on the western slopes was restored
The restorers tried to trace the peoples' descendants in the valley
They found none to bless the heiau's re-opening
On a Saturday morning as immaculate as Pele's mana
we stood in the heiau in their welcoming presence that stretched
across the valley and up into their mountains
where their kapa-wrapped bones are hidden

4.

The Ko'olau has seen it all
I too will go eventually
with my mountains wrapped up
in acid-free drawings that sing
of these glorious mountains
and the first Kanaka Maoli who named
and loved them forever

In Her Wake

I walk in her wake   almost every morning and afternoon
along the Mānoa Valley
from home and back after work
In her slipstream   shielded from the wind and the future
I walk in her perfume that changes from day to day
in the mornings with our backs to the Ko'olau
in the afternoons heading into the last light as it slithers
across the range into the west

She struts at a pace my bad left knee
and inclination won't allow me to keep up with
And when I complain she says   You just hate a woman
walking ahead of you
No   I hate talking to the back of your head

I'm the Atua of Thunder   she reminds me
when my pretensions as a Sāmoan aristocrat get out of hand
So kill my enemies for me   I demand
Okay   I'll send storms and lightning
to drown and cinderise them
Do it now   I beg

I can't I've got too much breeding to act like that
(How do you cure contradictions like hers?)

She loves Bob Dylan the Prophet of Bourgeois Doom
And this morning I swam in his lyrics as she marched ahead singing:
Sweet Melinda the peasants call her the goddess of gloom
She speaks good English
And she invites you up into her room
And you're so kind
And careful not to go to her too soon
And she steals your voice
And leaves you howling at the moon . . .

Yes for over a year I've cruised in her perfumed slipstream
utterly protected from threats
She'll take the first shot or hit in an ambush
And if a car or bike runs headlong into us
my Atua of Thunder with the aristocratic breeding
will sacrifice her body to save me

By the way she nearly always wears her favourite red sandals
as she like *Star Trek* forges boldly ahead singing Dylan songs
and me wanting to howl at the Hawaiian moon

She Dreams

Nearly always she remembers her dreams vividly
At breakfast this morning she recalled how she was flying
through a noiseless storm across the Straits for Ruapuke and her father
who was sitting on his grave in their whānau urupā wearing a cloak of raindrops
and she looked down and back at her paddling feet
and saw she wasn't wearing her favourite red sandals
She stopped in mid-flight in mid-storm and called Alapati get me my saviours!
Woke and didn't understand why she'd called them that

It's been about thirteen years and that makes you the man
I've stayed the longest with she declared unexpectedly
as we cleared the breakfast dishes
To her such declarations are so obvious and like raindrops
you can flick easily off a duck's back
but for me it will stay a nit burrowing permanently into my skin
I won't understand why

If I tell her that   she'll probably say   You love guilt too much
You read too much into things and need someone to blame
So shall I blame her for staying thirteen years and plus?
For not wearing her saviours and reaching her dead father
who would have taken off his fabulous cloak of rain and draped it around her?
Shall I blame her for not having met me when we were young
and we could have been together much longer?

Or shall I   as usual   just let it pass
content that I am blessed to be with her
and   in her dreams   one day she and I will fly together
through the voiceless storm to Ruapuke and her waiting father?
She will be wearing her saviours
and we will arrive safely

With Hone in Las Vegas

We're home   Hone   after four years in Hawai'i
but the winter cold is driving out the delicious warmth
of those islands from my bones

La'u uō   our lifelong addiction has been to gambling
not with money but with words and   though our winnings have been sparse
we've kept on playing
That's probably why I thought of you when Reina and I were in Las Vegas
for the first time a few weeks back
and I recalled your winter pilgrimage many years ago with your son down
from the Head of Māui's Ika   to Wanganui and up to Jerusalem
to farewell 'a tired old mate in a tent
laid out in a box
with no money in the pocket
no fancy halo, no thump left in the old
ticker'
Our trip though was not to a mate's tangi
but simply to visit a cousin and meet the Beast that is Vegas

At Honolulu Airport   beloved friends wished us well
and sent us on our way with their aloha

In summer   America is cocooned in air-conditioning
so when we unpacked like blind sardines out of the air-conditioned plane
and the Vegas airport terminal into the morning   the desert heat was

like raw buffalo hide tightening around us as it dried
and we blinked into thick bone-white air that smelled of dead fires and ash
Why had I expected Vegas to smell new and crisp?
And I remembered we agreed all our journeys are about other journeys
and through intricate layers of maps
Not just geographical/political/historical maps but those of
the moa and heart   dream maps   cinematic and literary maps
maps of pain and suffering   arrogance and deliberate erasures
maps which are the total of our cultural baggage
and in which we are imprisoned
and through which we read our elusive reflections
This trip wasn't any different

The luscious persuasive blonde at the Avis counter offered us
a GPS system and we took it – we'd not used one before
Out of all the maps I'd inherited of Vegas   I'd come to imagine
it a supersized civilisation created by a movie special effects genius
hired by hip gangsters   or conjured up by a gambler prophet hallucinating wildly
after fasting forty days and nights in the desert wilderness
But   as our GPS with the Maureen O'Hara voice piloted us
through gigantic rows of Casino and hotel billboards with gorgeous
Colgate smiles inviting us to dance forever with chance
through supersized developments   of new homes they couldn't sell –
the bottom had fallen out of the housing market –
through oases of grubby pawnshops and other businesses that picked
at the desperate bones of addicts
the hip maps began to vanish

When we checked into our Holiday Inn well away from the Strip
we were told our room wouldn't be ready until mid-afternoon
so in the blistering heat we went looking for food and found Sunset Station
and walked into all the clichés about Vegas casinos: cavernous palaces of perpetual
 air-conditioned night without time   peopled by exacting machines into
which mesmerised worshippers fed their adoration
gaming tables surrounded by narrow-eyed players totally in the zone
of the spinning wheel   or the flip of the card and the throw of the dice
The huge craziness of it was enthralling
Later as we sampled the Strip's mega megaresorts
with names straight out of Hollywood and the dream of gigantism
The Mirage
Wynn Las Vegas
The Sands
Treasure Island
The Golden Nugget

The Excalibur
The Luxor
The MGM Grand
Caesar's Palace
The Venetian
I recognised the Beast was indeed a creature
as magnificent as the Sphinx and the pyramids born out
of the Pharaohs' addiction to immortality
But this Beast was feeding off the insatiable American Dream
of limitless credit   choice and size
one press of the button   one spin of the wheel   one throw of the dice
and you're out of the desert forever

Every night   the porcelain moon over the city wore the Joker's cynical face
but a rescuing Batman wasn't anywhere in sight
as our cousin showed us how to play the machines
He played as if he was playing the piano and we tried to copy him
as we slotted in our money and lost and lost but I didn't care
because I kept hoping for that buzz that radiates through
my veins when I'm gambling with words that shape
fabulous beasts out of the deserts of ourselves
But auē Hone   the buzz never came
and I found gambling for money sadly   sadly boring
Definitely not my choice of addiction

The tangata whenua have been written out of Vegas' history
On our last night   as we and our cousin and other relatives gorged
on a lush buffet at a Japanese restaurant   they told us of Hawaiian friends
who'd just walked off a building site because three of their mates
had been killed there in terrible accidents
When they'd started bulldozing the site   one of the Hawaiians   a kahuna
had sensed the enormous disquiet of the spirits of the tangata whenua
who   he believed   were buried there
and had asked their white bosses to stop the project
and let him perform the rituals of appeasement and cleansing
They'd refused and within three days their friends were dead

The next morning   in light as brittle as salt   Reina   my beloved tautai
drove us out of Vegas and we headed for the Grand Canyon and Santa Fe
in the arid heart of America
But that's another story   Hone   for another winter day

Garden 4

in memory of Epeli Hau'ofa

In Kyoto many years ago I discovered there are no shadows in traditional Japanese paintings
In this midday light the bare rotary clothesline in our backyard can't cast a shadow
Our house was rented out for four years and in July we returned from Hawai'i to winter
and an overgrown backyard hedge garden lawn and wet clayey soil that stank
In front of the lanai someone had planted a small patch of strawberries
Locked in the suffocating shadows of the border trees my mandarin tree was dying

With gifted hands and devotion Reina pruned weeded and planted
Now the new garden is thriving in the summer wet and heat
and honeybees hum as they feed on the nectar of the rainbow flowers
as if this lush growing and harvest will last forever

My daughter Mele emailed this morning to say Epeli had died in Suva
Last year he and Ngũgĩ and I were to give a joint reading in Honolulu
He couldn't make it because he had to come to Auckland for cancer treatment
Amuia le masina e alu ma toe sau . . .

Garden 5

for Caleb Alualu

Every time Caleb our 8-year-old mokopuna stays with us
he tries to win Manoa's affection but she won't have any of it
For the last two days his father has pruned and cut down some of
our overgrown trees while three teenage mokopuna and I piled up
the cut trunks branches and foliage into large mazes Manoa explored
oblivious to the pungent smell of drying timber and leaves
and Caleb's desperate attempts to befriend her
My daughter Sina came for morning tea on the lanai: coffee crispies
and fruit mince pies while Caleb tracked the heartless Manoa through the mazes
The sun hid behind a mattress of milk-white cloud that stretched over
the city and up to Waitakere and refused to help Caleb

Reina keeps telling him the next time he comes Manoa won't spurn
his alofa: cats are cats and you just have to wait for them to trust you
Unlike humans they're very honest about their feelings

Garden 26

in memory of Alistair Te Ariki Campbell

While we were having breakfast this morning   National Radio
announced that Alistair had died after a long illness
We visited him last year in his house which is perched above Pukerua Bay
defying the storms   as it gazes out at Kapiti – Te Rauparaha's fortress now bird
sanctuary which Alistair loved and turned into the haunting songs of 'Sanctuary of Spirits'
Meg had died a few months before so he was still in mourning
moving gingerly round his house as if even the air was hurting

He made us tea and wanted to know about the years we'd spent in Hawai'i
He reciprocated by telling us about Meg's death and how he missed her
Later he took us into his study and gave us copies of his collections
to select from for our anthology *Mauri Ola*

As we were leaving he led us into the fierce wind and his garden at the edge
of the precipice and pulled out three young aloe vera plants for us to take home
Today   despite the winter   those plants thrive in our garden

A Definition of Atua, from *The Adventures of Vela*

Atua are rooted in the soil bed of the heart
in our terrible dreams that search to vine
us to Varinomino where we began

Atua to explain the tides that flow in our blood
and connect us to the weeping moon
and the pain of flesh and bone

the reason in the wind's unpredictable curve
and the silence that weaves all things
in the paradigm we must discern

the wherefore in the dragonfly's midair hover
and in the surgreen depths of the sea
eating the new leaf vein by living vein

Atua are our reflections becalmed in
the hurricane's eye
to blame for our madness our inability
to LOVE

('A Definition of Atua'
from *The Adventures of Vela*)

Wendt
Powrowley 09

Cave of Prophecies, from *The Adventures of Vela*

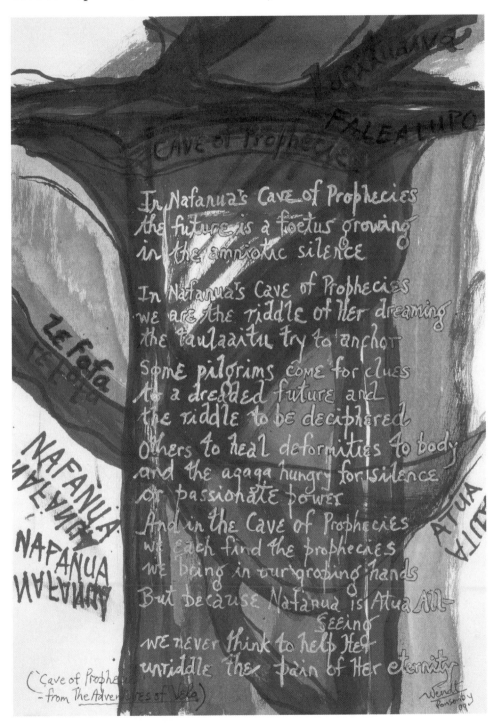

In Nafanua's Cave of Prophecies
the future is a foetus growing
in the amniotic silence

In Nafanua's Cave of Prophecies
we are the riddle of Her dreaming
the taulaaitu try to anchor

Some pilgrims come for clues
to a dreaded future and
the riddle to be deciphered
Others to heal deformities to body
and the agaga hungry for silence
or passionate power
And in the Cave of Prophecies
we each find the prophecies
we bring in our groping hands
But because Nafanua is Atua All-
Seeing
we never think to help Her
unriddle the pain of Her eternity

('Cave of Prophecies
- from The Adventures of Vela)

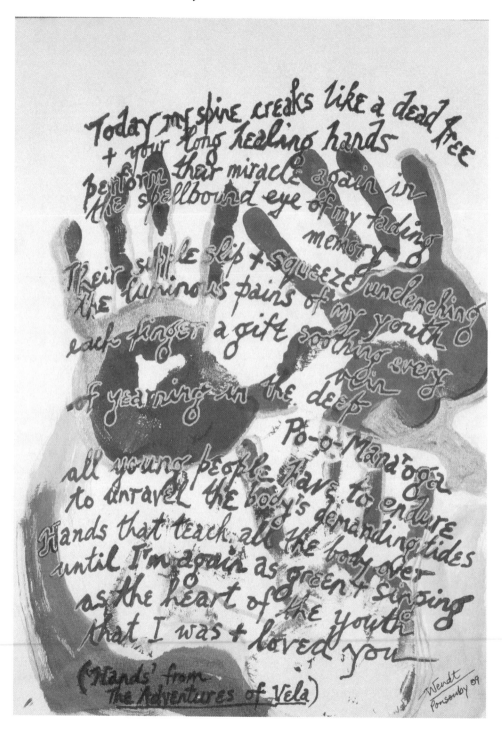

Today my spine creaks like a dead tree
+ your long healing hands
perform their miracle again in
the spellbound eye of my fading
                    memory

Their subtle slip + squeeze unclenching
the luminous pains of my youth
each finger a gift soothing every
            hair
of yearning in the deep

                    Pō-o-Manaʻōga
all young people have to endure
to unravel the body's demanding tides
Hands that teach all the body over
until I'm again as green + singing
as the heart of the youth
that I was + loved you

('Hands' from
The Adventures of Vela)

Wendt
Ponsonby 09

Galulolo

WAYNE KAUMUALII WESTLAKE

Wayne Kaumualii Westlake (1947–1984) was born on Maui and raised on the island of Oʻahu, where he attended Punahou School. He also studied at the University of Oregon and earned his BA in Chinese studies at the University of Hawaiʻi. Westlake broke new ground as a poet, translated Taoist classical literature and Japanese haiku and interwove perspectives from his Hawaiian heritage into his writing and art. He published his substantial body of work locally, regionally and internationally and when he died prematurely in 1984 he was at the height of his poetic career. A long-overdue volume of his work, *Westlake: Poems by Wayne Kaumualii Westlake*, was published by the University of Hawaiʻi Press in 2009.

Statehood

15 years today
    since STATEHOOD
it's raining
i feel like
       crying

Huli

"Huli"   W. Westlake '79

Down on the Sidewalk (in Waikīkī)

down on the sidewalk
in waikīkī
I
  SEE
      EVERYTHING
passing me:

lost souls
girls with nice asses,
businessmen
      with dirty assholes
      and shiny suits,

bums   pimps   whores
freaks   junkies   gigolos
and burnt out Amerikans . . .

they're
straight   bent
slimy   clean
women under the
      spell of the MOON
children learning
      the GAME too soon

policemen   hippies
kahunas (a few)
fat sick Amerikans
and speedy Japanese

studs   cunts
rich   poor
perverts   weirdos
beggars   fools
crazy-men
and old people
      about to DIE . . .

they're all there
i tell you,
      man
from my seat

down on the sidewalk
in waikīkī
I SEE EVERYTHING:
this gigantic PIG
                    PARADE
          staggering by . . .

and across the street
unnoticed,
an old Hawaiian
      slowly sweeps
    the sidewalk
                clean
        with a fallen
        coconut leaf:

away,
          you fools
      he whispers,
                    away!

The Kahuna of Waikīkī

the bum Hawaiian
came up to me
down on the sidewalk
in waikīkī
put out his hand
said he needed smokes
asked me for
some change

i reached in my pocket
looking for the cash
asked how he was doing

the World these days
SO STRANGE –
  'gotta know where
  they are first
  before they know
  where you are'

he said, 'I could
go home RIGHT NOW!'

paranoid looking around
wanting to leave
i gave my last dollar
to the kahuna of waikīkī
mumbling INSANELY
stumbling down
the crowded street . . .

As Rats Climb the Coconut Trees

waikīkī
         with all its people
     is still
            a lonely place

as rats climb
the coconut trees
                  the meat
keeps broiling and
       fat pigs still
                  slide out of
         cadillacs
                  OINKING
fingering the slimy
         green GOD
     of waikīkī:

'the whores don't
       want your cock, man
they want your
       MONEY!'

. . . as rats climb
the coconut trees
                  going insane
down on the sidewalk
                  in waikīkī i
       remember the kahuna
how he treated

                pretty girls:
swatted them away
                    like flies!

i stumble sad
            and lonely
down the crowded
               streets

. . . as rats climb
the coconut trees . . .

The Hawaiian

down on the sidewalk

in waikīkī

the old Hawaiian

                  kept looking

            up in the sky

i wondered

       why?

what's he looking

           at?

looked up to see

mynah birds frolicking

          in coconut

               trees

of course!

of course!

Pakalolo

LOLOLOLOLOLOLOLOLOLOLO
LOLOLOLOLOLOLOLOLOLOLOLO
LOLOLOLOLOLOLOLOLOLOLOLO
LOLOLOLOLOLOLOLOLOLOLOLO
LOLOLOLOLOLOLOLOLOLOLO
LOLOLOLOPAKALOLOLOLOLO
LOLOLOLOLOLOLOLOLOLOLO
LOLOLOLOLOLOLOLOLOLOLO
LOLOLOLOLOLOLOLOLOLOLO
LOLOLOLOLOLOLOLOLOLOLO
LOLOLOLOLOLOLOLOLOLOLO

Native-Hawaiian

how we spose
feel Hawaiian anymoa
barefeet buying smokes
in da seven
eleven stoa . . . ?

VERNICE WINEERA

Of Ngāti Toa and Ngāti Raukawa descent, Vernice Wineera grew up in Takapūwāhia Pā, Porirua. She studied at BYU-Hawaii in Laʻie, Hawaiʻi, and gained her MA and PhD in American studies from the University of Hawaiʻi. Her poetry has appeared in anthologies and journals in New Zealand, the South Pacific and Hawaiʻi and the mainland United States. Her books include *Mahanga: Pacific Poems* (1978), *Ka Poʻe o Laie* (1979) and *Into the Luminous Tide: Pacific Poems* (2009). She served as a vice president of the Polynesian Cultural Center (1980–92), and worked at BYU-Hawaii, first as editor of the university magazine (1978–80) and later as director of The Pacific Institute (1992–08). Now retired, she is working on a series of contemporary Pacific paintings exploring the landscapes of her heritage anchored in Te Moana Nui a Kiwa.

Boy in a Sleeping Bag

First he lays it flat along the ground,
making sure there are no rocks beneath.
Then, legs together, sliding carefully,
he inches between its quilted folds,
aware that any jut of knee
or elbow will disturb
the perfect symmetry
that is his private bed.
Once in,
he reaches sleepy fingers
to tug the awkward zip
up to his chin.
One last glance beneath the chairs
assures him that there are no bears
then, snug and warm in his bright cocoon,
my son camps out in the living room.

BRIAR WOOD

Briar Wood grew up in Māngere in Auckland, and is currently a senior lecturer at London Metropolitan University. She is a graduate of the University of Auckland and has a DPhil from the University of Sussex. Her poetry and critical writing have been widely published. In 2001 she wrote poems for the *Glorified Scales* installation by Maureen Lander at Auckland War Memorial Museum, which referred to their Ngā Puhi whakapapa.

Ship Girl

Custom Street on Friday night
dressed up to meet the blokes,

summer down The Waterfront –
with a new pack of smokes.

My idea of bright lights
K Road in the pouring rain.

Rulers of the Queen Street scene –
in only the flashest of bars

we're speaking tima mole creole
checking out fresh sailors

under the southern stars.
They have a good Jack nohi

believe me. Regulars
might buy a pretty sexy dress

so I impress his mates.
But if he's sleazy

us two do a runner –
we laugh and laugh, comparing notes.

That merchant navy chap
with a tattooed cartoon of me

on his freckled back
likes his bottom well smacked.

I get regular injections
to keep clear of infection.

You know that expression
the oldest profession?

Not easily shocked, me.
The Tokyo marine who

had a pearl inserted that rotates
at the tip of his cock.

No need for pimps
and no scrimping

I'm going to buy myself
a nice flat in Herne Bay.

Live with my son and mother.
I'll get legit. Yeah. Really. One day.

Glossary

a hui hou	(Hawaiian) until we meet again
'a'ā	(Hawaiian) roots
'A'ala Honua	(Hawaiian) sweet-smelling land
'a'ama	(Hawaiian) a species of black, edible crab
'afakasi	(Sāmoan) part European
afio mai lau afioga a Tuātagaloa	(Sāmoan) welcome, your lordship, Tuātagaloa
agaga	(Sāmoan) soul
ahi kā	(Māori) refers to a person's right to land as long as they maintain their presence or home fire
'āholehole	(Hawaiian) a particular silver-coloured reef fish
'ahu	(Hawaiian) altar
ahunga nui	(Māori) provider of plentiful food
'ahu'ula	(Hawaiian) feather cape or cloak
'ai kae	(Sāmoan) eat shit
āiga	(Sāmoan) family, extended family
'āina	(Hawaiian) land or earth
aitu	(Sāmoan) spirits
ali'i	(Hawaiian / Sāmoan) chief
alu su'esu'e	(Sāmoan) go and do your research
'alualutoto	(Sāmoan) blood clot; premature baby
amuia le masina e alu ma toe sau . . .	(Sāmoan) envy the moon, it goes and returns . . .
'anae	(Sāmoan) mullet
aoa	(Sāmoan) banyan tree
'a'ole pua	(Hawaiian) lit. 'without flowers'; in genealogies, a line without children
'apa i'a	(Sāmoan) tinned fish
'apa supakeki	(Sāmoan) tin of spaghetti
arero	(Māori) tongue
aroha / alofa / aloha	(pan-Polynesian) unconditional love, compassion, caring and concern; the ability to accept another reality without condemning it or trying to change it
atua	(Māori / Sāmoan) god/s
'auala	(Sāmoan) road
auē! oi auē	(Sāmoan) alas! woe is me
'aumakua	(Hawaiian) ancestral gods, family gods, in animal form
auoia	(Sāmoan) expression of surprise
'auwai	(Hawaiian) waterway, canal
'avapui	(Sāmoan) bitter ginger
'awapuhi ke'oke'o	(Hawaiian) white ginger
billi billi	(Fijian) bamboo raft
bua	(Fijian) frangipani or plumeria flower
bubu	(Fijian) grandmother
bure	(Fijian) house
coco-kava	kava mixed with cocoa
dalo	(Fijian) root vegetable
e ala e	(Hawaiian) rise up
e hoa / e hoa mā	(Māori) friend / friends
e kala mai	(Hawaiian) excuse me

e kelē le kamāloa	(Sāmoan) the man is big (as in status, standing)
e ki, e ki, waiho o maunga	(Māori) shame! let your mountains
e mau ka Maoli!	may the indigenous people of Hawai'i continue/endure!
e tumu i le fa'aaloalo	(Sāmoan) full of respect
'ei	(Cook Island Māori) garland of flowers
'ekahi	(Hawaiian) one
'ele'ele	(Sāmoan) earth, soil
'elepaio	(Hawaiian) species of flycatcher; also a variety of taro
'elua	(Hawaiian) two
fa'asāmoa	Sāmoan way
fa'afāfine	(Sāmoan) the way of a woman; cognate with the classic Tongan word 'fakafafine' and related to the eastern Polynesian word 'mahu'. It refers to the practice of biological men living as women in Sāmoan culture. By 'woman' one means actually a 'femme' or 'feminine'. Fa'afāfine do not identify as women or as gay men but as their own people
fa'amolemole	(Sāmoan) please
fa'i	(Sāmoan) banana
faigāmalaga	(Sāmoan) journey
fale	(Sāmoan) house
faleuila	(Sāmoan) toilet
fanua	(Sāmoan) land
fetu tasi, lua, tolu, fa, lima, ono, fitu	(Sāmoan) star one, two, three, four, five, six, seven
filemū Sāmoa	(Sāmoan) peace Sāmoa; quiet Sāmoa
frangipani	pan-Pacific tropical flower
gogo	(Sāmoan) long-tailed tropical bird
gogolo	(Sāmoan) rumbling
hā	(Hawaiian) breath
ha'u kai	(Tongan) come and eat
haka	(Māori) fierce, energetic, dance; used to challenge the enemy and inspire young men prior to battle or encounters with strangers
hale	(Hawaiian) house
hāngī	(Māori) earth oven
haole	(Hawaian) a white person; any foreigner
hāpai	(Hawaiian) carry
hei paepae kōiwi, whare tipuna!	(Māori) be charnel houses, houses for the ancestors!
heiau	(Hawaiian) a temple of worship
hīkoi	(Māori) a protest march; to walk or protest
hīnaki	(Māori) eel pot
Hinemoa	Māori woman of legend; Hinemoa and Tūtānekai were two lovers who would meet on the island in the middle of Lake Rotorua
ho'okupu	(Hawaiian) gift; lit. 'to activate growth'
hongi	(Māori) traditional greeting; to share the breath of life by pressing noses
hori	colloquial word for Māori
hui	(Māori) meeting of the people, gathering; people coming together
hula	(Hawaiian) dance of Hawaiians
huli	(Hawaiian) to turn
huni	a small coastal tree, the flowers and leaves of which are used in garlands and to scent Tongan oil
huruhuru	(Māori) feathers, hair

ia manuia lau faigamalaga	(Sāmoan) have a safe journey
'iao	(Sāmoan) bird
'ie lavalava	(Sāmoan) sarong, wrap-around garment
Iesu Keriso ma lona tinā	(Sāmoan) Jesus Christ and his mother
ihu	(Māori) nose
'ili'ili	(Hawaiian) pebbles
'ili'ili hānau o Kōloa	(Hawaiian) birth stones of Koloa
i mua! i mua!	(Hawaiian) advance!
inamona	(Hawaiian) condiment made from kukui
inoa pō	(Hawaiian) dream name
ipo	(Māori) sweetheart, lover
ipu	a gourd, or a drum made from a gourd, that accompanies Hawaiian chant and dance
'iva / 'iwa	(Hawaiian) frigate bird
ivi	(Sāmoan) bone/s
iwi	(Māori) tribe; bone/s. The bones of the dead, considered the most cherished possession, were hidden. The iwi contains the mana of an individual even in death
Jack nohi	(Māori, colloquial) nosey parker
ka moauli	(Hawaiian) the dark blue sea; short for moana uli
ka Pākīpika	(Hawaiian) the Pacific
ka pō a me ke ao	(Hawaiian) night and day
ka pouli	(Hawaiian) dark night
ka tangi te tītī	(Māori) the tītī bird cries; first half of a well-known tauparapara or chanted opening to a formal speech on the marae
kahu	(Māori) cloud
kahuna	(Hawaiian) one of the priestly caste
kai	(Māori) food, to eat; (Hawaiian) ocean/tide
kaitiaki	(Māori) guardian
kakala	(Tongan) garland, or a collection of fragrant parts of a plant, especially flowers
kalepe	(Sāmoan) to break apart
kalo	starchy tuber that is the staple of the Hawaiian diet; metaphorically, kalo is the parent of the Hawaiian people
kanae	(Hawaiian) fringe-lip mullet
kanaka	(Hawaiian) people
Kanaka Maoli	Hawaiian people
kani	(Hawaiian) sound
kanikapila	(Hawaiian) to play music together
kapa haka	(Māori) traditional songs/dances
kapa	(Hawaiian) cloth made from pounded bark, usually from wauke or mamaki bark, and imprinted with intricate designs; clothes
kape	(Cook Island Māori) a root crop, member of the taro family
kapu	(Cook Island Māori) sacred, holy
karakia	(Māori / Cook Island Māori) prayer, poem or incantation
kaula	(Hawaiian) rope
kaumātua	(Māori) male elder/s versed in the traditions, histories and practices of the ancestors
kava	(pan-Polynesian) pounded root; ceremonial drink
kawa	(Māori) protocol
kēhua	(Māori) ghost/s; spirit/s
kei hea a Tāmaki-makaurau?	(Māori) where is Tāmaki-makaurau?
keiki	(Hawaiian) child

kete	(Māori) basket, kit
kia ora	(Māori) informal greeting, lit. 'be well'
kiekie	(Māori) a plant used for weaving
kina	(Māori) sea-urchin, sea-egg
kino lau	(Hawaiian) term for the many forms taken by a god, such as the ti leaf as a form of the mo'o (lizard) god
koa	(Hawaiian) brave; warrior; large, native Hawaiian forest tree with crescent-shaped leaves, which produces a fine red hardwood formerly used for canoes, now for furniture, calabashes and 'ukulele
ko'ako'a / ko'a	(Hawaiian) coral
koe ha mea fia ma'u?	(Tongan) what is that you are trying to find?
kōhanga reo	language nest; total immersion Māori pre-schools that were established to save te reo Māori
koko alaisa	favoured Sāmoan dish made of rice, coconut milk and cocoa
kōrero	(Māori) speech, conversation
kōrero neherā	(Māori) ancient stories
korokoro	(Māori) lamprey
kōwhai	New Zealand tree with yellow flowers
ku'i	(Sāmoan) hit, punch
kua riro nei a Maungawhau, Maungarei, Ōrākei!	(Māori) Maungawhau, Maungarei and Ōrākei are lost to us!
kuapā	(Hawaiian) wall of a fish pond
kui lei	(Hawaiian) to string flowers, beads, shells into a lei
kuia	(Māori) senior woman, female elder
kukui	(Hawaiian) candlenut tree; candlenut; lamp
kūmara	(Māori) sweet potato
kupe	(Sāmoan) money
Kusaie	Kosrae, Federated States of Micronesia
kūtai	(Māori) mussels
la'u uo	(Sāmoan) my friend
Laka	Hawaiian goddess of the forest and green things, sister of Pele
lali	(Sāmoan) large wooden gong
lanai	(Hawaiian) balcony, veranda
lau pisi!	(Tongan) silly show-off!
lavalava	(Sāmoan) wrap-around garment
le anae oso o fiti	(Sāmoan) the jumping mullet of Fiji
le āva o i'a eva	(Sāmoan) the bay of wandering fish
le fale o Maka	(Sāmoan) the house of Maka
lei	(Hawaiian) garland of flowers
lei pīkake	(Hawaiian) a lei of pīkake flowers
leo pa'ulua	(Sāmoan) voice out of tune
lia hiwa ra	(Hawaiian) be alert
Lili'uokalani	last reigning monarch of Hawai'i before its annexation by the United States
limu	(Hawaiian) general name for all plants living under water, salt or fresh
lo'i	(Hawaiian) paddy, swamp
lo'i kalo	(Hawaiian) paddy gardens for growing taro
loco moco	Hawaiian dish of rice, gravy and fried egg
lokelani	(Hawaiian) heavenly rose
loko i'a	(Hawaiian) fish pond
lulu	(Sāmoan) owl
mai ke po'o a ke kapua'i	(Hawaiian) from the head to the feet

maika'i	(Hawaiian) good; a good thing
maile	a Hawaiian twining shrub with fragrant, shiny leaves used for decoration and lei, reserved for the highest ceremonial occasions or honours
maka	(Tongan) rock
makeki	(Sāmoan) market
makeki fou	(Sāmoan) new market in central Apia
mamae	(Māori) sadness; hurt; pain
mamalu	(Sāmoan) dignity; prestige
mana	(pan-Polynesian) miracle; presence; spirit; divine power, authority; prestige; inner strength
mana'o	(Hawaiian) thought, idea, belief, expectation
manu	(pan-Polynesian) bird
manuhiri	(Māori) visitor/guest
mānuka	New Zealand tea-tree
Maoli	indigenous people of Hawai'i
Māori	indigenous people of New Zealand
marae	(Māori) short for Te Marae-atea a Tumatauenga, meaning the space immediately before the wharenui or meeting house; now used to refer to the entire complex, usually consisting of a wharenui (meeting house), wharekai (dining hall) and wharepaku (ablutions block)
marangai	(Cook Island Māori) east southeast wind
masi	(Fijian) bark cloth
Matariki	(Māori) Pleiades constellation; new year celebration
Mau	Sāmoan independence movement against New Zealand occupation
Māui	pan-Pacific trickster demi-god
Māui-a-ka-malo	(Hawaiian) Māui of the loincloth
Māui-tikitiki-a-Taranga	(Māori) Māui who was found floating on Taranga's topknot
mauka / maunga	(Hawaiian / Māori) mountain
meaalofa	(Sāmoan) gift
mihi	(Māori) speeches of greeting and introduction
mo'o	(Sāmoan) gecko
mo'o'ōlelo	(Hawaiian) story, myth, legend; literature
Mo'okū	(Hawaiian) priest of the war god
mo'okū'auhau	(Hawaiian) genealogy
moa	(Sāmoan / Hawaiian / Māori) chicken; centre, heart; extinct bird of Aotearoa
moki	(Māori) trumpeter fish
moko	(Māori) facial tattoo
moko, mokopuna / mo'opuna	(Māori / Hawaiian) grandchild
moso'oi	a Sāmoan tree that produces fragrant yellow flowers used for lei and for scenting coconut oil
motokā	(Māori) car
motu tapu	(Māori) sacred islet
muliwai	(Hawaiian) end water
Muriwai	(Māori) one of the seven wives of Tangaroa
nā 'ōiwi	plural form of native, or native son; the bones; refers to the indigenous people of Hawai'i
nā'au	(Hawaiian) lit. 'intestines', 'bowel'; refers to the mind or heart, the place where one senses one's kupuna or ancestors
na'auao	(Sāmoan) learned, intelligent; knowledge
Nafanua	Sāmoan goddess of war
nau mai	(Māori) welcome
ngākau	(Māori) seat of affections; heart; mind; eager, all fired up

nifo'oti	(Sāmoan) long knife used in knife dance
nīkau	(Māori) type of tree
niu	(pan-Polynesian) coconut
Niu Sila	(Sāmoan) Aotearoa New Zealand
noa	(Māori) free from tapu, ordinary, of no consequence
nonu	(Sāmoan) tree that bears a fruit used for medicine
nui	(Māori) big, large
o ka pō	(Hawaiian) of the night
'O le tala i tufuga o le va'a o Tagaloa	(Sāmoan) the story of the builders of Tagaloa's sailing craft
O le tamāli'i	(Sāmoan) the aristocrat/chief
'O le to'o savili, 'o le sa'o fetalai	(Sāmoan) the voice of the wind, the ali'i who speaks
'oha	(Hawaiian) taro corm
'ohana	(Hawaiian) family
'ohe	(Hawaiian) bamboo
oli	(Hawaiian) chant
'olo	(Sāmoan) fort or shelter
olonā	(Hawaiian) fibrous plant used to make white cordage
'ōpae	(Hawaiian) shrimp
'ōpū	(Hawaiian) stomach
ou, ou, ou e, te vaine Anami	(Cook Island Māori) oh, oh, oh, those Anamese women; from a popular Cook Island song praising the beauty of women from Vietnam
pā	(Māori) fortified village
Pa Ariki	one of the traditional chiefs in the Takitimu district in Rarotonga
pa'akai	(Hawaiian) salt
pa'umuku kirl	(Sāmoan) prostitute girl, slut
pa'u-stina	(Sāmoan, colloquial) prostitute
pai	(Cook Island Māori) good; a banana and arrowroot flour pancake commonly made in Ma'uke
pakalōlō	(Hawaiian) cannabis
pākau	(Māori) kite
Pākehā	(Māori) New Zealander of European descent; non-Māori New Zealander
pālagi	(Sāmoan) a white or Western person, a person of European descent; lit. 'from the clouds'
palusami	Sāmoan delicacy made of young taro leaves cooked in coconut cream and onions
pandanus	a pan-Pacific tree, the leaves of which are soaked in the sea and dried in the sun for mats, baskets, etc.
papakāinga	(Māori) village, home place
papa ku'i	(Hawaiian) board for pounding poi
patē	(Sāmoan) small wooden drum
paū	(Sāmoan) ominous
paua	a variety of New Zealand shellfish, abalone
pe'a	(Sāmoan) flying fox; male body tattoo
Pele	Hawaiian goddess of volcanoes, a major deity
pelu	(Sāmoan) shortened form of sapelu, bush knife
pepe	(Sāmoan / Māori) baby
pīkake	the Arabian jasmine, introduced to Hawai'i from India. Its very fragrant small white flowers are often used for lei and other decorations
piko	(Hawaiian) navel cord, navel
pilau	(Hawaiian) stench, rot

pilikaki	(Sāmoan) tinned pilchards
pipi	a variety of New Zealand shellfish; fledgling
pisupo	(Sāmoan) canned corned beef
pito-pito	(Māori) the remainder of the umbilical cord that finally falls off a new baby's belly-button
pō	(Māori / Sāmoan) night
pōhaku ku'i 'ai	(Hawaiian) stone food pounder
poke	(Hawaiian) marinated raw fish
poki	(Sāmoan) slap
popo	(Sāmoan) coconuts
pōtiki	(Māori) youngest child of a family
pōuliuli	(Sāmoan) dark night
pounamu	New Zealand greenstone found in Te Waipounamu (the South Island)
pōwhiri	(Māori) the process by which people are welcomed on to a marae or any other place in which the welcome rituals are observed
pua	(Sāmoan / Hawaiian) flower
pua'a	(Sāmoan) pig
Puanga	(Māori / Cook Island Māori) the star Rigel
pueo	Hawaiian owl
pūhā	edible New Zealand plant, the sowthistle, rich in iron and vitamin C
puka	(Hawaiian) hole
pūkana	(Māori) fierce facial contortion where the tongue is extended
puke	(Māori) hill; navel
puletasi	(Sāmoan) two-piece garment for women
Pulotu	Sāmoan spirit world
puni kālā	(Hawaiian) greedy; greediness
pūpū	(Hawaiian) shells
pute 'oso	(Sāmoan) protruding navel
rakoa	white-tailed tropical bird
rangatahi	(Māori) young people
rangatira	(Māori) person of high rank, chief, leader
raukura	(Māori) feather, plume
roimata	(Māori) tears
rou rou	(Fiji) leaves from dalo plant
ruruhau	(Māori) shelter
sa'o lelei	(Sāmoan, colloquial) that's right
saka	(Sāmoan) boiled food
Sāmoa mo Sāmoa	Sāmoa for Sāmoans
sapasui	Sāmoan chop suey
Saveasi'uleo	Sāmoan half man, half eel who was the father of Nafanua and guardian of Pulotu, the spirit world
sega	Sāmoan parakeet
siapo	(Sāmoan) bark cloth
sina	(Sāmoan) silver-haired with age
sio lalo	(Tongan) look down on
Sisu Kalaisi	(Tongan) Jesus Christ
susu	(Sāmoan) breast; milk
ta'amū	(Sāmoan) giant taro that must be properly peeled to avoid burning and itching of the mouth and tongue
Tagaloaalagi / Tagaloa	Sāmoan creator god, supreme ruler
tākapu	(Māori) gannet
Takitimu	one of the great canoes that arrived in Aotearoa

Takurua	(Māori / Cook Island Māori) Sirius, the Dog Star
tala	(Sāmoan) story
talanoa	(Sāmoan) to discuss
talavou	(Sāmoan) youth
talie	(Sāmoan) almond tree
talofa	(Sāmoan) greetings
tama āiga	(Sāmoan) of kingly or high chiefly status; son of a high-ranking family
tamakeu	(Cook Island Māori) traditional title
tāne	(Māori / Sāmoan) husband, man
Tangaroa	Māori god of the sea
tangata enua	(Cook Island Māori) people of the land
tangata fanua o Sāmoa	people of Sāmoa
tangata whenua	(Māori) inhabitants of a specific place; people of the land
tangi	(Māori) cry, weep, mourn; funeral
tangiwai	(Māori) a kind of greenstone found in the Milford Sound area
tanifa	(Sāmoan) the white shark
taonga	(Māori) treasure; something of value
tapa	(pan-Polynesian) beaten bark cloth
tapu	(pan-Polynesian) sacred, holy; worthy of deep respect
taro	(pan-Polynesian) a starchy tuber that is the staple of the diet of many Polynesian people; metaphorically the taro is the parent of the Hawaiian people
taro lo'i	(Hawaiian) taro paddy, a swamp where taro is grown (lo'i taro)
tatau	(Sāmoan) tattoo
taufale	(Tongan) broom
taupou	(Sāmoan) leading maiden in the village, usually daughter of ali'i
tautai	(Sāmoan) navigator
Tāwhirimātea	Māori god of winds and storms
Te Moana Nui a Kiwa	(pan-Polynesian) the mighty ocean of Kiwa, the Pacific Ocean
te reo	the Māori language
Te Rerenga Wairua	(Māori) place where the souls of the dead depart for Hawaiki
teina	(Māori) youngest sibling, junior relative
tēnā koe	(Māori) greeting to one person; hello; lit. 'is that you?' or 'there you are'
ti	(Hawaiian) a long-leaved plant
ti'otala	(Sāmoan) kingfisher
tieke	(Māori) saddleback bird; also a transliteration of 'check'
tihei	(Māori) exclamation of approval
tihei mauri ora	(Māori) I sneeze, it is life
tiko	(Māori) excrement
tinā	(Sāmoan) mother, used as the title for elderly ladies
tipuna / tīpuna	(Māori) ancestor/s, male or female; see also tupuna / tūpuna
tīwī	(Māori) television
toetoe	(Māori) plant with long, grassy leaves with a fine edge and saw-like teeth. Flowers are white, feathery, arching plumes
tohu	(Māori) sign, symbol
toto	(Māori) blood
Tu	Māori god of war
tuatua	a variety of New Zealand shellfish
tufuga	(Sāmoan) master tattoo maker, master craftsman
Tuhei	current Māori chief / leader of the Waikato tribes
tui	(Māori) native songbird with a white tuft at its throat and two voice boxes; also a popular brand of New Zealand beer
tuku iho	(Māori) handed down through the generations

tukutuku	(Māori) woven reed panels on the walls of meeting houses
tūpāpaku	(Māori) deceased, corpse
tupu'aga	(Sāmoan) origins, source
tupu'aga o le āiga	(Sāmoan) ancestors and/or descendants
tupuna / tūpuna	(Māori) ancestor/s; Western dialect variant of tipuna
tusili'i	(Sāmoan) fine or wavy lines used to connect individual designs and spaces in siapo
tūtae	(Māori) faeces
Tūtānekai	Māori man of legend; Hinemoa and Tūtānekaiwere lovers who would meet on the island in the middle of Lake Rotorua
tūtū	(Hawaiian) grandparent/s; elders
tu'ugamau	grave
ua pala le ma'a, ae le pala le upu	(Sāmoan) the stone wears away, but the word doesn't
ua sā	(Sāmoan) sacred; keep out; forbidden
ua uma le Mau	(Sāmoan) the Mau is over
'ukulele	(Hawaiian) stringed instrument; flying flea
uliuli	(Sāmoan) black
'ulu	(Hawaiian) breadfruit
ulu	(Hawaiian) head
Uluhaimalama	(Hawaiian) Queen Lili'uokalani's garden
uri	(Māori) descendants, offspring, progeny
urupā	(Māori) burial grounds, cemetery
va	(Sāmoan) space between
vaka / va'a	(Cook Island Māori) canoe, sailing vessel
vakalolo	(Fijian) dessert made with coconut and taro
vao	(Sāmoan) forest
vi	Sāmoan fruit tree
vi'ia le Atua mo Sāmoa e	praise be to God for Sāmoa
Viti	Fiji
vu ni yalo	(Fijian) ancestral spirit
vuni-vasa	(Fijian) a sacred place
wahine / wāhine	(Māori) woman / women
wahine kapu	(Hawaiian) sacred woman
wai	(Hawaiian / Māori) water
waiata tangi	(Māori) lament
waiata	(Māori) to sing; song
wairua	(Māori) spirit, soul
wairua tapu	(Māori) sacred spirit
waka	(Māori) vessel; often used to refer to one of the great ocean-going vessels that brought the ancestors of Māori from islands in the Pacific to Aotearoa New Zealand; see also vaka
wana'ao	(Hawaiian) dawn
whakaaraara	(Māori) to alert, awaken; sentinel's chant
whakapapa	(Māori) genealogy
whakataukī	(Māori) proverb, wise and pithy saying
whānau	(Māori) extended family
whānau urupā	(Māori) family cemetery
whare	(Māori) house
whare whakairo	(Māori) carved meeting house
wharepuni	(Māori) principal house of a village; guest house; sleeping house

Index of titles

Index of poets by country